# The Leadership Secrets of Genghis Khan

www.rbooks.co.uk

*Also by John Man*

Gobi: Tracking the Desert
Atlas of the Year 1000
Alpha Beta
The Gutenberg Revolution
Genghis Khan
Attila
Kublai Khan
The Terracotta Army
The Great Wall

JOHN MAN

# THE LEADERSHIP
# SECRETS OF
# GENGHIS
# KHAN

BANTAM PRESS

LONDON · TORONTO · SYDNEY · AUCKLAND · JOHANNESBURG

TRANSWORLD PUBLISHERS
61–63 Uxbridge Road, London W5 5SA
A Random House Group Company
www.rbooks.co.uk

First published in Great Britain
in 2009 by Bantam Press
an imprint of Transworld Publishers

A CIP catalogue record for this book
is available from the British Library.

ISBN 9780593062029 (cased)
9780593058480 (tpb)

Addresses for Random House Group Ltd companies outside the UK
can be found at: www.randomhouse.co.uk
The Random House Group Ltd Reg. No. 954009

The Random House Group Limited supports The Forest Stewardship
Council (FSC), the leading international forest-certification organization. All
our titles that are printed on Greenpeace-approved FSC-certified paper carry
the FSC logo. Our paper procurement policy can be found at
www.rbooks.co.uk/environment

Typeset in 11/14.5pt Century Schoolbook by
Falcon Oast Graphic Art Ltd.

Printed and bound in Great Britain by
Clays Ltd, Bungay, Suffolk

2 4 6 8 10 9 7 5 3 1

Mixed Sources
Product group from well-managed
forests and other controlled sources
www.fsc.org   Cert no. TT-COC-2139
© 1996 Forest Stewardship Council
FSC

# Contents

Preface   vii

Introduction: On Leadership, and What It Means   1
1   Character: The Roots of Leadership   13
2   Warlord: How to Make a Nation   43
3   Reformer: The Founding Father   65
4   Commander: First Steps in Empire-Building   79
5   Strategist: Expansion Westward   98
6   Sage: The Search for Ultimate Truths   123
7   Conspirator: The Last Campaign and Death   138
8   Legacy: Failure, Collapse and a Memory of
     Glory   150
Appendix: Getting the Measure of Genghis's
     Genius   162

Bibliography   172
Index   177

# Preface

THE LEADERSHIP 'secrets' in this book are keys to what made Genghis great. Obviously I do not claim that Genghis himself should be a model for leaders today, in business or government or criminal gangs or any other group. Given the unique nature of his times, his circumstances and his personality, it would be ridiculous to do so.

But some aspects of his leadership have relevance today. Take the simple guidelines adopted by a friend of mine who is a leading figure in the private, public and voluntary sectors. Advice, study and experience have reduced his leadership principles to six simple points:

1  Vision: define and articulate clearly where you want to go.
2  Get the right people; and get rid of the wrong ones fast. Then . . .
3  . . . delegate, delegate, delegate.
4  Be consistent on the main points, but flexible on details.
5  Reward success.
6  Deal ruthlessly with failure; do it fast; and learn from it.

That's it. Easy to say, hard to achieve. Everything else, he says, is fine-tuning.

You will find all six of these points embedded in Genghis's style of leadership. But there was also much more to him, for no one these days has to juggle life and death and conflicting principles and novelty as he did. His world was a precarious one of shifting alliances, in which trust was vital; but so, occasionally, was treachery. To win trust and justify

treachery, he needed magical social skills. And a high, yet
flexible, sense of morality. With your very life at stake, with a
nation's fate in the balance, is loyalty, which you proclaim as
your highest virtue, always going to determine your actions?
What, for instance, if you see that it has become necessary to
execute your greatest friend, which is not a circumstance confronted by many leaders today? What happens to your principles
when you move up from level to level of leadership, from clan
chief to tribal ruler to king to emperor, while playing the overlapping roles of social reformer, general, strategist and judge?

If you ask what was Genghis's most remarkable asset, I
think it was this: that he was one of the few leaders who are
exceptions to the Peter Principle. This states that people get
promoted for competence and stop being promoted when they
prove incompetent; therefore, given time, all organizations
tend towards incompetence.[1] On the contrary: at every level
in his rise, Genghis acquired new competence. It was this
supreme skill, combining so many others – learning, posing
new questions, devising solutions, moving on upwards – that
marks him out as a genius.

So Genghis's life story does not contain a recipe for successful
leadership. At best, among his responses to the challenges he
faced, *some* leaders *may* spot *some* things which *may* suggest
skills that *may* apply in the world today. As team leader, CEO,
commander, strategist, school head or any other of the countless
roles that demand leadership in modern life, you will have to
make your own decisions about which, if any, of Genghis's
skills you might learn from. I can only present evidence, and
a few judgements. It's you who must do the real work.

---

[1] In the words of the principle: 'in a hierarchy every employee tends to rise to his level of
incompetence'. See Peter and Hull, *The Peter Principle*. 'Peter's Corollary' is that 'in time,
every post tends to be occupied by an employee who is incompetent to carry out his duties'.

# INTRODUCTION:
# ON LEADERSHIP, AND WHAT IT MEANS

I F EVER I make a film on my subject, it will start with the camera tracking over open grasslands, along a broad river, over a ridge, up a steep-sided valley to a shoulder-muscle of rock and forest. Words appear on screen:

NORTHERN MONGOLIA, 1181

We zoom into forest, to the figure of a man in wrap-around coat leading a horse uphill through firs made sparse by wind and altitude. When he glances round, his face shows him to be young, around 19 or 20. He's sweating, panting, afraid, and we understand why: from below come voices. Subtitles translate: *He must have gone this way! No, that! See the hoofprints!*

The young man is, of course, the future Genghis Khan. Right now he is khan of nothing and no one. He doesn't yet have his famous name. He is Temüjin, a fugitive on a remote mountain, fatherless, the son of an outcast mother, a young man with high ambitions, but now apparently facing imminent death.

Yet in 20 years he would unite Mongolia, in another 20 he would rule much of Asia as khan of the greatest land empire in history. And that was only the start. His heirs doubled this estate, giving his grandson Kublai, emperor of

China, nominal authority over one-fifth of the world's land area. That's quite a leap in three generations.

To conceive of the impact Genghis Khan had upon the world, imagine this:

In the 1870s, Geronimo unites the North American Indians. He seizes arms, devises new tactics, destroys wagon trains, defeats the armies of the post-bellum United States. He directs his armies, now reinforced with white troops, westward to California, eastward to New York and Washington. Canada falls. With the wealth of the north behind him, he turns on Mexico, then in another brilliant campaign pushes north, through Alaska, and on over the Bering Strait into Siberia. By the turn of the century, all the Americas and a good deal of Russia are ruled by a man born into an unknown clan of unlettered, feuding Indians. China prepares for war. European powers humbly seek accommodation.

To both Europeans and Chinese alike, at the opposite ends of Eurasia, the Mongols sprang out of the dark under a leader who seemed as impossible then as an Apache in the White House in 1900. Their success had much to do with their toughness, ruthlessness and self-sufficiency as mounted archers. But they had been tough, ruthless and self-sufficient for centuries. That they were able to explode from their grassland home was due entirely to the qualities of their leader, one of the most astonishing personalities in history. Once historians debated whether great historical shifts were caused by inevitable forces – social pressures or climate changes – or by personalities. For those who believe, as the nineteenth-century British historian Thomas Carlyle did, that history was 'at bottom the History of . . . Great Men', Genghis is a prime example.

His empire lasted for 140 years after his death, then it too died, not with a bang but with a long-drawn-out whimper, leaving traces that were visible for centuries. They are still obvious today. Genghis's grandson was Kublai Khan, who conquered China and established a Chinese dynasty, the Yuan. His conquests extended the old Chinese heartland to include Yunnan and Tibet, and also to reassert possession of the far west, Xinjiang. It was Kublai, therefore, who defined the limits of modern China. This is one of the oddest consequences of the Mongol empire: that China owes its geographical self-image to the ambitions of an impoverished young Mongol fleeing for his life on the flanks of a Mongolian mountain.

It has to be asked: How on earth did he do it? And why?

## Genghis as leader: time to reassess

This book grew out of a brief, tongue-in-cheek analysis of Genghis Khan's leadership in a previous book, *Genghis Khan: Life, Death and Resurrection*. But if Genghis was, as I believe, among the greatest leaders in history, then his skills deserve a more serious approach. What drove him? What traits did Genghis possess, exactly? How did they develop? Were they unique, or might some of them be universal?

*What drove him? What traits did Genghis possess, exactly? Were they unique, or might some of them be universal?*

Until recently, these questions were almost impossible

to answer. A classic study of Genghis's conquests in north China, written in 1950, begins with these words: 'Neither in the past nor present has any historical figure excited greater admiration, fear and hate than Chingis Khan,[1] but of few such men have we so exasperatingly little detail and authentic information.'[2] But that was before any good modern edition of the Mongols' foundation epic *The Secret History of the Mongols*, and before the emergence of leadership theory. Armed with these two tools, it is now possible to propose answers.

It's a good time to do so. For Mongols, Genghis is of unique significance, because they look upon him as the founder of their nation. Though officially frowned on during seven decades of Communism, he remained an unofficial object of adulation. Now he is more revered than ever. Shrines to him are not uncommon. I once saw a portrait of him drawn by a teenager pinned up among the family photographs in a *ger*. Attempts to get at the 'real' Genghis are often seen as disrespectful. Those – mainly foreigners – who search for his tomb are regarded with intense suspicion. Genghis intended his grave to be kept secret! His wishes must be honoured! In the most recent Genghis film, Sergei Bodrov's *Mongol*, nominated for an Oscar in 2008, the lead is taken by a Japanese actor, Tadanobu Asano, to the initial horror of Mongols. Luckily, Asano's startling looks, brilliant acting and linguistic skills (he learned Mongol for the part), and

---

[1] 'Chingis' should be the standard transliteration, with the *ch* as in 'church'. 'Genghis' derives from the French, which pronounces the *Ge-* soft, like the *s* in 'pleasure'. English-speakers hardened the sound to the *g* in 'good'. That's wrong, but it's an uphill struggle to correct both spelling and pronunciation. Pending change, it's OK to pronounce him with a *dj* sound, like the *Ge-* in 'George'.

[2] Martin, *The Rise of Chingis Khan*.

Bodrov's own obvious respect for his subject, did a good deal to swing opinion around.

Yes, now is a good time to take a deeper look at Genghis. Why did he set out on his career of conquest and domination? And how? And what did he have that made him so appealing to his people and so successful?

First the 'why?', because it is fundamental to everything else. Why would an illiterate nomad wish to force his immediate neighbours into alliance, then turn them against his more distant neighbours? There are two answers: emotion and politics. A peculiar combination of circumstances and character planted in him a passion to build security. The only way to do this was to escape the destructive round of blood-feuds that had always hampered Mongolia's nomadic clans and tribes – feuds that the settled cultures south of the Gobi exploited to keep the 'northern barbarians' weak, 'using barbarians to control barbarians', as the urbanized southerners put it. A few previous leaders had achieved partial unity, enough to wring booty from the settled cultures; but always some nomadic tribes had been left out, and the feuds, with their brief and self-serving alliances, prevented any more genuine unity emerging. Genghis – and only Genghis – saw that the way to a better life was to manipulate established tribal traditions, seize control of the system, shatter it and create a new type of entity, which would then be used to achieve security and wealth on an unprecedented scale. This was a planned agenda, ruthlessly executed. In the words of the great Mongolist Owen Lattimore, 'All his moves were politically calculated, and the calculation, from early in his career, was directed towards the building of a structure of power that would be capable of extension in both time and space.'[2]

As for the 'how?' – well, that's what most of this book is about. If it is a good time to seek answers to questions about Genghis because of his renewed popularity, it is doubly so because leadership theory is all the rage. There are books by the score on the good and bad habits of leaders, on their secrets, levels, dimensions, qualities and faculties, often precisely numbered, all promising stunning insights. I have selected what seem to be the most helpful approaches,

*'All his moves were politically calculated, and the calculation, from early in his career, was directed towards the building of a structure of power that would be capable of extension in both time and space.'*

and used them to spotlight Genghis's achievements. He remains in some ways unique, as you would expect for an obsessive empire-builder who exploited mass murder as a strategic weapon. But there are aspects of him – character traits, choices, patterns of behaviour, strategic decisions – that fit many aspects of modern leadership theories, whether corporate, political or military.

So here is a portrait of Genghis as leader, drawn from historical sources – chiefly the Mongols' foundation epic, *The Secret History* – but also from other contemporary records, and from anthropology and psychology. Into this portrayal I have woven those aspects of modern leadership theory that seem most appropriate. My aim is to open the

[2] *Scientific American*, August 1963.

way to anatomize the qualities of this most ambitious, ruthless, brilliant and supremely successful of leaders.

## On the nature of leadership

Before turning to the roots of Genghis's leadership qualities, we should know what we mean by 'leadership'. In this vast and slippery subject, one thing most agree on is that 'true' leadership differs from both the exercise of power and the art of management. 'Power grows out of the barrel of a gun,' as Mao observed, but also from many other advantages – physical strength, class, inherited wealth, electoral victory: whatever its base, it is not necessarily the same as leadership. As James MacGregor Burns argues in his massive *Leadership*, the book that made leadership studies into an industry, tyrants are not 'proper' leaders because they use force. Nor is management to be equated with leadership, because to manage is to cope with lesser matters arising from the flow of events or past leadership decisions. 'True' leadership must surely involve an element of persuasion on the leader's side and choice by followers: a would-be leader fails if possible followers run in the opposite direction or, in the case of medieval Mongolia, gallop off to join some other leader.

Leadership nowadays is usually assessed in positive terms, as if it were all about doing good. It's the leaders who persuade, who take the route of peace, democracy and non-violent competition, who are 'proper' leaders. They, after all, are the most numerous and influential in a world of democracies and corporations. It's their skills the world needs, their skills we should be studying, their qualities we should focus on when assessing a leader like Genghis.

But hold on a minute. That's modern, western-style corporate leadership. Taking a wider view, leadership cannot be entirely separated from the exercise of power. There was once a strand of leadership theory according to which power, ruthlessly sought and ruthlessly exercised, is the bottom line, for without it there can be no true leadership. It was this philosophy that lay behind the two rulers who most effectively imposed China's unity: the First Emperor in 221 BC and Mao Zedong in 1949. Both would have approved of Machiavelli, who, when confronted with Renaissance Italy's warring mini-states, argued that without the ruthless – indeed, cynical; even deceptive – exercise of power there is no state, no guarantee of peace, no possibility of progress. In this view leadership is power.

Often with dire consequences. Historically, there have been countless appalling leaders who have brought about extreme suffering and destruction. As Harvard's Barbara Kellerman reminds us, bad leadership is as valid a subject as good, the one casting light on the other. Genghis ranks among the bad as well as the good, with the destruction of dozens of cities and the deaths of millions of people (over 3 million in eighteen years, at a rough guesstimate) to his debit. No assessment of his leadership can ignore this aspect of him. It would be easy to condemn, and leave things there. But it should be remembered, first, that his attitudes were of his time; he managed to do what countless lesser despots aspired to, and failed to achieve. Second, these were not inexplicable, random acts of racist rage; they were the consequences of careful thought. An explanation is possible, and I have attempted to provide one.

Some tyrants may be born to tyranny; others resort to it when their powers of persuasion fail. These bad guys were once good guys, admired at home and abroad, until events and hindsight and corruption and personality cults and quirks of character turned them into devils. Does that make any one of them less of a leader in the early stages? As Barbara Kellerman asks, who says that to persuade millions to go to war is less of a talent than to lead them to peace? That the release of evil is less worthy of study than the release of good?

If this is so, then goodness and badness, virtue and vice, are not fundamental elements in leadership. They are secondary elements, which emerge only when a leader is in power. But how does he or she achieve power, assuming it is not simply inherited? Not through some leadership gene that preordains dominance. Every alpha male has to win his position. We should be starting with something even more basic, the power to achieve power, the power of *persuasion*. But, since there's not much point in persuasion that leads nowhere, we must focus on persuasion that actually works; on *effectiveness*.

We should first ask: What means does a would-be leader, in this case Genghis, use to weld a group or groups together and motivate them? It's not enough to say he appealed to their self-interest, their greed or their need for security, because these drives had always been there. There is something even more fundamental. 'Great leadership works through the emotions,' as Daniel Goleman writes. It's that primal emotional appeal that needs explanation to

*What means does a would-be leader, in this case Genghis, use to weld a group or groups together and motivate them?*

start with. Only then should we ask: how effective was he? And how was he effective?

The root of that fundamental appeal must lie in some quality, or qualities, of the leader's character. It has become a cliché of leadership theory that the quality we should be looking for is 'charisma'. Originally, a charisma (or 'charism', as the *OED* puts it, without the '-a') was any 'gift or favour specially vouchsafed by God; a grace, a talent', such as the power of healing or prophecy. It has the same root as 'charity', the divine gift of generosity. It was the German political philosopher Max Weber (1864–1920) who popularized the word as the quality 'by virtue of which [a person] is set apart (originally by prophets, healers, law-givers, hunting-leaders or war-heroes) and seen as possessing supernatural, superhuman, or at least in some way exceptional powers or qualities not available to anyone else. These powers are regarded as of divine origin or as exemplary, and on this basis he is treated as "leader".'[3] Weber went on: 'How the quality in question would be objectively judged from an ethical, aesthetic, or other such point of view is naturally indifferent for the purpose of definition.' So there are two problems with charisma: it is a gift, magically and inexplicably conferred; and it may be used for good or ill. The word provides no basis for judgement. Moreover, if it is magical, or the result of divine inspiration, it explains nothing. It's tautological: 'He's a leader because he's a leader.' What we are after is understanding: *how* does a leader become a leader, acquire charisma? This is the rock-bottom question,

---

[3] *Wirtschaft und Gesellschaft* (1922), publ. in English as *Theory of Social and Economic Organization* (1947): see ch. 3 on 'The Nature of Charismatic Authority and its Routinization'.

our starting point for understanding Genghis's rise.

Only then can we analyse the way Genghis used his power; how, in Joseph Nye's words, he managed to combine *soft power* (persuasion) and *hard power* (coercion) to achieve the *smart power* that allowed him to transform his society and create something new in human history.

## On being great

Another theme that will emerge from this analysis is the idea of greatness in leadership. We shall look at effectiveness in its many manifestations, and at goodness and badness, with all the advantages of hindsight; but there have been many effective leaders, bad and good, who have not qualified for greatness. Greatness in leadership involves some form of creativity, which initially comes from within as a *vision* of change. That vision must be *pursued*, and finally *achieved* (at least in part), making something for followers that was not there before – *transformation*, in the current jargon. All this implies an assessment of what change meant, a before-and-after view of the context in which Genghis operated. What was the nature of the society that formed him? What was special about his circumstances? Was change coming anyway, and he merely a leader who rode the wave of change? Or was he the instrument of change? As we shall see, on this basis Genghis qualifies for greatness on many counts.

Consideration of what it is to be a great leader returns us to the question of morality. Does greatness necessarily involve doing good? Obviously not, for in rapid change – change effected by one person over a few years – some will suffer. But that is no reason to condone the imposition of suffering. Genghis was and is a hero and a saint to his own people, a mass murderer with no redeeming features to his victims. And his vision of universal rule, so appealing to his people, was in the end completely batty, as his grandson Kublai discovered when he failed to conquer Japan, Java, Burma and Vietnam, let alone anywhere further afield. It was a fantasy, in pursuit of which Kublai set his dynasty on the road to ruin. Morality shifts with time and place, good slides into evil; but we should at least raise the issues, and see if we can come to some new conclusion.

The conclusion I hope to show is that Genghis was a great leader – one of the greatest, despite the evil he did – because of his many positive qualities, which is why he is a heroic figure in both Mongolia and China. For instance, he, of all people, had the opportunity to profit from his conquests. Yet he did not, at least not in a personal way. He was uncorrupted, inspirational, open-minded, curious, generous, persuasive, and many other things as well. These are rare qualities in a despot – and they are what make him worth studying.

GENGHIS'S LEADERSHIP:
KEY ELEMENTS TO BE EXAMINED
**Context 1**: what formed him
**Context 2**: what he wanted to change
**Vision**: what he wanted to achieve
**Persuasion**: the tools he deployed
**Charisma**: the nature of his appeal
**Character**: the nature of his personality
**Effectiveness**: what he achieved
**Morality**: what was good, what was bad
**Greatness**: assessing his achievement

# 1

# CHARACTER:
# THE ROOTS OF
# LEADERSHIP

T HE CAMERA is still on Genghis's face. A voice comes distantly from below: *Oh, leave him, he'll die anyway.*

Well, no, he won't. He is well prepared for survival: a bow slung from his belt, a quiver full of arrows, a leather flask of fermented milk. As the voices fade, his expression changes, to relief, then determination. He knows this place from childhood, for he is on the sacred mountain of the Mongols. Burkhan Khaldun, as it came to be called, Sacred Khaldun, is the heartland of his people, who had settled here some 500 years before. He finds a deer-trail, follows it downhill, comes to a clearing overlooking the river that has its source here, and sets about building a shelter of branches torn from the willow bushes that cover the lower slopes.

Three days later, friends tell him the coast is clear. He is overcome with gratitude for his survival. This is not the first time he has found shelter from enemies in the woods and defiles of Burkhan Khaldun, but never before has he had such a close call. It seems to him there must be more than skill and good luck involved.

He believes – no: he *knows* – he is in divine hands.

To us today this sounds a little crazy. But for the Mongols 800 years ago this conviction of divine support was the source of Genghis's power, his charisma. Indeed, many still believe in it today; they pray to his spirit in a temple to him, the so-called Mausoleum of Genghis Khan, near Dongsheng in Inner Mongolia. Of course, for non-Mongols interested in the nature of leadership, it is no explanation at all. We see it as a consequence of his appeal, not its cause. Before looking more deeply at the nature of that appeal, we have to understand why and how he could claim divine backing, and why he was taken seriously.

## Charisma and divine backing

As pastoral nomads, the Mongols practised a religion rooted in the natural world. There are no records of pre-thirteenth-century practices, but it is possible to strip away the Christian, Daoist and Buddhist elements of later centuries to focus on the ancient fundamentals of their nature-religion, shamanism. Traditionally, herding life was dominated by the great bowl of the sky, the endless steppe and weather that can suddenly turn brutal. Winter temperatures can plunge to −50°C, ice may brick over the winter grass and kill cattle by the million, and life depends precariously on good summer pastures. The supreme power, Blue Heaven – Khökh Tenger – also known as Eternal Heaven, controlled all, dealing out random disaster and munificence, working through lesser spirits in rivers, springs, thunder, fire, sun, wind, rain and snow. By Genghis's time, contact with other cultures had revealed to the Mongols that their Tenger was, in essence, the same god as the Chinese Heaven (tiān /天), the Christian God, the Muslims' Allah, a being whose wishes could be understood and who could be persuaded to help humans if approached with the correct prayers and rituals. Shamans could get close when they donned their masks, sounded their rattles and drums and entered trances that took them to the realms of the ancestors and spirits. Ordinary people, too, could hope to get a sense of Tenger if they climbed the highest mountain peaks.

Now (to return to our opening sequence) Genghis, like Moses on Sinai, is up there on the Mongols' most sacred mountain. He has no need of shamans. He can claim direct contact with his god on high. He vows he will honour the mountain always as the place of his deliverance by remembering it in his prayers every morning, as his children will, from generation to generation. Facing the rising sun, he drapes his belt around his neck and removes his hat, the traditional way of deferring to a higher power. He beats his chest and kneels nine times towards the sun, scattering mare's milk with flicks of his fingers.

How do we know this? We don't absolutely, for he was the only source. No one else was with him for those three days. But he gave a version of events to close friends who were nearby, checking that it was safe for him to reappear. People talked, and spread the story, and recorded it, in memory and words and music. The Mongols did not yet know how to write, so there were no written records. But they had a long musical tradition – a century later, Marco Polo recorded how Mongols prepared for battle: 'then might you have heard a sound arise of many instruments of various music, and of the voices of the whole of the two hosts loudly singing' – and an equally long bardic tradition. In the words of the eminent Mongolist John

Krueger, of Indiana University: 'One may safely assume
. . . that epics existed for some hundreds of years, purveyed
solely by oral means.'[1] Imagine bards weaving stories
about Genghis into long songs, short songs, epics,
stories and legends, using families of fiddles, flutes and
percussion instruments and employing a range of vocal
techniques, like the combination of deep-note drone and
nasal whistle known as overtone or throat singing.

## The Secret History and its agenda

No writing means no hard evidence, but it is fair to infer
the existence of oral tales and songs from the first book in
written Mongol, *The Secret History of the Mongols*, the
only near-contemporary account of Genghis's life, reflect-
ing the 'pure, unmitigated tradition of the nomadic tribes
of Mongolia'.[2] Its theme is Genghis's Heaven-backed rise
to empire. *The Secret History* was probably conceived, and
possibly written, when the Mongol leaders gathered in
central Mongolia in 1228 to confirm the succession of his
heir, his third son Ogedei. Such an occasion, with family
members, clan heads and their people coming together
from all over Central Asia and north China, would have
been an ideal time to gather the tales that the bards were
singing. One-third of the *History* is in alliterative verse,
some of it densely poetic, rhythmical language that empha-
sizes incidents and speeches of particular importance. It is
'the work of a people still in the dawn of their poetic
creativity', as John Krueger puts it, something between

---

[1] Krueger, *Poetical Passages in the Erdeni-yin Tobāi.*
[2] De Rachewiltz, *The Secret History.*

history and epic, between prose and poetry, packed with incidents carefully selected as milestones in Genghis's ancestry and development.

It is important to remember that *The Secret History* reflects the way Genghis wished himself to be presented. Some tales must surely have been discouraged or suppressed by him and his adoring heirs. It is, if you like, the medium through which he spun the image of himself. It should be welcomed as crucial evidence, but with a high degree of scepticism about its face value. When these events cast him in a less-than-perfect light, well, that was what he wanted – to be seen as a man backed by divinity, not as divine himself. With that warning, the evidence can be used to deduce much about his character: this was a man not blinded by his own talents, content to have some faults revealed; a leader keen to present himself as vulnerable, just like any ordinary man, but as possessing the strength and talent to overcome that vulnerability. (As a child, we are told, he was afraid of dogs; quite right, too, for Mongolian dogs were – and still are – bred big and aggressive to fight off wolves and scare the wits out of thieves.) He was no democrat; but he was no crude despot, either. Obedience was won in exchange for brilliant leadership. This was, as Mongols still assert today, sometimes with religious intensity, a hero in whose service was perfect freedom.

On Burkhan Khaldun, Genghis completes his obeisance. Forty years later, when *The Secret History* came to be written, an unnamed bard put Genghis's feelings into verse:

*A shelter of elm twigs*
*I made my home.*
*Thanks to Burkhan Khaldun*
*I escaped with my life, a louse's life.*
*Fearing for my life, my only life,*
*I climbed Khaldun*
*With one horse, following elk tracks;*
*A shelter of broken willow twigs*
*I made my home.*
*Thanks to Burkhan Khaldun*
*My life, a grasshopper's life,*
*Was indeed shielded!*[3]

He comes down, rejoins his family, starts on the long, hard road to national unity and empire. Somewhere along the way, during the transformation of the 20-year-old down-and-out into the 60-year-old conqueror, his followers came to believe that, as national founder and empire-builder, he was fulfilling Heaven's will. That is how *The Secret History* presents him. Its first sentence proclaims that his original legendary forefather had been 'born with his destiny ordained by Heaven Above'. Indeed, it soon became accepted that Genghis's family was actually related to God through a Mongol version of the Immaculate Conception: 'Every night,' says one of the ancestral mothers, explaining how she became pregnant with three of Genghis's forefathers, 'a resplendent yellow man entered by the light of the smoke-hole or the door-top of the tent, he rubbed my belly and his radiance penetrated my womb. When he departed, he crept out on a

---

[3] All quotes from *The Secret History* are from the de Rachewiltz translation.

> ### GENGHIS'S LEADERSHIP SECRET NO. 1
>
> ## CONTROL THE MESSAGE
>
> From ritual to spin-doctoring, presentation has always been a crucial element in leadership. In Genghis's case, he had to rely on his heirs. *The Secret History*, written shortly after his death, was crafted by an anonymous author to present Genghis's central message: that he was the instrument of divine will. In the *History*, he implies he was sustained by this belief even before he began the 20-year task of unifying the Mongol tribes. Perhaps it was true. Anyway it worked. In the words of Joseph Nye, 'A good narrative is a great source of soft power.'

moonbeam or a ray of sun in the guise of a yellow dog.' The idea of divine support is repeated many times: according to a stock phrase in edicts by Genghis and his heirs, he acts 'under the protection of Eternal Heaven'. The impetus to assert divine backing may have come from him, or it may have been suggested by others and allowed by him. It hardly matters which. The point is that during his life it became an article of faith, a vital aspect of his leadership.

But to what end? In Christian theology, Jesus is not just the Son of God. He is the Son of God for a purpose: to redeem the world. The big idea in *The Secret History* was that Genghis was destined by Heaven to unify the two main rival Mongol clans, then the neighbouring Mongol- and Turkic-speaking groups, then the more distant tribes of the Mongolian west. These would become 'his people'. At their head he would eventually go on to create an empire, and to claim a yet greater destiny: to rule the world. Or rather, not so much claim a destiny as act out a truth that would become manifest to other peoples as the empire grew. When the Mongols reached Europe, almost 20 years after Genghis's death, his grandson and the third khan, Güyük, wrote to Pope Innocent IV, 'Through the power of God, all empires from sunrise to sunset have been given to us, and we own them. How could anyone achieve anything except on God's order?'

So to Mongols of the time this was the self-evident sequence:

HEAVEN'S WILL

*leads to*

GENGHIS'S LEADERSHIP

*leads to*

UNITY AND CONQUEST

The logic will hardly appeal to non-Mongols. The reasoning is circular: Heaven chooses Genghis, Genghis's success proves he is fulfilling Heaven's will. For those of us who seek more persuasive cause-and-effect explanations, there is no point in Heaven choosing a leader unless the leader has the character to put Heaven's will into effect. So in our search for explanation, it is character that must come first, which is then accepted by his people, producing this sequence:

CHARACTER

*leads to*

PERSUASION

*leads to*

GROUP ACTION

*leads to*

UNITY AND CONQUEST

Luckily, the writers and editors of *The Secret History* also had a feel for historical and psychological explanation, and provide us with evidence. Heaven's will needed to be implanted in a character 'with strength', i.e. one formidable enough to realize that will. So what were Genghis's initial strengths, his character traits? How were they formed? What drove him to unify his clans, found a nation, build an empire?

## The right man for the right time

Great leaders do not spring from nowhere. They arise in response to urgent problems. If there aren't any, visionaries and would-be leaders end up muttering their dreams in back streets and asylums. A nation has been defeated, and a Hitler rises to capitalize on failure. A nation faces defeat, and a Churchill steps forward to inspire resistance. So it was with the Mongols.

In about 1130, three decades before Genghis's time, his great-grandfather Kabul had become the first ruler of all the Mongols, heading a steppe federation that, to us with the benefit of hindsight, foreshadows nationhood. It didn't last. The Mongol-speakers were nomads and herders, which made them, in Chinese eyes, mere barbarians – but dangerous ones, who would, if they could, plunder the farming, urbanized people to the south of the Gobi desert. So when the chance came, in about 1164, north China, at that time the separate state of Jin, scattered the nomad tribes, making enemies here and alliances there: in a stock phrase of the time, 'using barbarians to control barbarians'. Mongolia fell back into clannish anarchy and fratricidal warfare, with every local ruler jockeying for the loyalty of young bloods and the friendship or defeat of rivals. Every man and woman, every family, had their bonds, but all had to reach out on occasion – for pastures, trade goods, marriage partners – and test the dangerous borders beyond which the ties of family and friendship no longer held and enmity loomed. A young man might pledge himself to a leader; friends might swear eternal brotherhood. But pledges and oaths could evaporate. A chief who could no longer guarantee protection and booty would see his disgruntled power base vanish across the steppe. This was the violent and chaotic world into which Genghis was born. The times were ripe for a leader; the people were ready to be led.

*The times were ripe for a leader; the people were ready to be led.*

And, given unity, they had the means to conquer. They knew that with their nomadic ways they could be far superior to the urbanized peoples living south and east of the Gobi. Even today, Mongols – at least those raised in the countryside – are among the toughest people on earth. Taught to ride as soon as they can walk, they grow up used to privation. In the long-distance horse races held on national sports days in July, ten-year-olds ride bareback for 25 kilometres or more. As adults, their livelihood will depend on their horse-borne herding skills. Once, they shared with other nomadic pastoralists the supreme skill of horseback archery. In disciplined formation, mounted archers could run rings round peasant foot soldiers and princely chariots – 'to such an extent', as the military historian John Keegan writes, 'that we may regard the steppe nomads as one of the most significant – and baleful

– forces in military history'.[4] When, in response, Chinese rulers adopted the ways of the pre-Mongol 'barbarians' (actually, the Xiongnu, often for dubious reasons called Huns), the barbarians still had the advantage because they could disperse like smoke across their open plains and go on living, as they always had, on their own simple resources: grass, water, meat, wool, furs. Despite occasional, disastrously expensive, victories by the Chinese, one great truth about the history of north China for 2,000 years was that the nomads and the Chinese occupied different universes, with the northerners free to roam and attack at will, while the Chinese retreated behind their city walls, and their Great Wall. (Actually, the Wall was an artificially clear-cut, and always permeable, barrier across a swathe of overlapping ecologies – desert, river, grassland and farmland.) Population pressure from China has gradually pushed the boundary between the two cultures northward, until today it lies several hundred kilometres north of the Great Wall.

## Boyhood: the formative years

So Genghis, born around 1162 and hearing as he grew up tales of what his great-grandfather had achieved, would have been aware that life did not have to be an endless round of cattle-raiding, wife-stealing, revenge-killing and deprivation. With the right leadership, unity was possible; and wealth was there, to the south, for the taking.

The child is often father to the man, in this case the future leader. In an article in the *Harvard Business Review*

[4] Keegan, *A History of Warfare.*

devoted to leadership, the psychoanalyst Manfred Kets de Vries comments:

> Once I started, I found that business leaders were much more complex than the subjects most psycho-analysts studied . . . They can't be too crazy or they generally don't make it to senior positions, but they are nonetheless extremely driven people. And when I analyse them, I usually find that their drives spring from childhood patterns and experiences that have carried over into adulthood.[5]

Little Genghis – Temüjin, as he was known before he became khan – was his parents' eldest child. Having become expert on horseback by the age of four, he would soon have been responsible for important tasks around the *ger*: herding the 'five animals' (sheep, goats, cattle, horses and camels), collecting dung for fuel and (in winter) ice to make water, controlling the dogs, guarding against wolves, taming foals, learning to wrestle and shoot and to hunt marmots and butcher sheep. (Mongols have an efficient technique for this last task, which involves tipping the sheep on its back, making a little incision in the chest, inserting a hand and grabbing the heart to stop it. It sounds nasty, but in fact sheep, once inverted, are remark-ably compliant, and the operation seems to cause no pain.) Killing animals was utterly, unsentimentally routine, which made pastoralists equally adept and unsentimental about killing humans. The work allowed little relaxation, except in late July and August when the herds were fat on

---

[5] Coutu, 'Putting Leaders on the Couch'.

summer grass. The extended family of grandparents, parents, four other children, servants and, in this case, a secondary wife,[6] plus her two children, would have been a tight-knit community, reaching out to other groups to exchange food, animals and clothing. The family was relatively well-off, being descendants of a khan, and its status was assured by Temüjin's father, Yisügei. Of aristocratic blood, he was a famous warrior who had successfully raided an enemy tribe to the east, the Tatars, just before his son's birth. Indeed, his son had been named Temüjin after a captive Tatar chief. The boy would have been raised with as much security as anyone could expect in an insecure world.

But at the age of nine he discovered just how bad things could get. His father, having just placed him with the family of his future bride – these matters were decided by parents, years before the wedding – was poisoned on the way home by enemies, Tatars from Manchuria (in vengeance for raids like the one in which Yisügei had captured Temüjin's Tatar namesake). The leader of another related clan, the Taychiuts, seized control. Temüjin's mother, Hoelun, was left without a protector, and with seven children (five of her own, two by the second wife). Rather than commit the crime of murdering a high-born family, the Taychiuts abandoned the widow of the dead khan, seizing her herds and leaving her and her offspring to die from cold and starvation. But they survived – just. For a few crucial years, young Genghis knew what it was to live without a network of kin, without animals to provide meat, milk or felt for a new *ger*

---

[6] A woman named in other sources as Suchigil, about whom *The Secret History* says little.

covering, longing for the freedom of the steppe and for security.

At this point, let's pause to examine what these devastating experiences – his father dead, his family rejected, his world shattered – might have meant to a young boy.[7]

Until recently, if asked to imagine the impact on a nine-year-old of such emotional blows, many psychologists would have considered a string of reactions almost inevitable: depression, antisocial behaviour, feelings of guilt, suicidal tendencies or ideas, the collapse of relationships with friends. Not so now, and not so in twelfth-century Mongolia. A number of psychological studies have backed the common-sense opinion: that given the right circumstances, children of eight or over can and do mourn a father's death in healthy ways. Genghis knew the dangers of steppeland life, and would have been well prepared for the stages now recognized as important for healthy grieving: acceptance of death, freedom to acknowledge rather than suppress the pain of loss, an ability to re-adjust, a readiness to preserve the memory of his father. He would have been 'resilient', in a term favoured by modern psychologists. Here are some of the traits identified in a range of studies that tend to 'promote resilience':[8]

- problem-solving skills;

---

[7] *The Secret History* says he was nine. As Mongols count, you are one at birth, which makes him eight in western terms. But nine has symbolic significance. He could have been a year or two older (not younger, because his baby sister, the fifth child, was still 'in the cradle' at the time.
[8] Summarized in Hurd, 'A Teenager Revisits her Father's Death'.

- social competence;
- a sense of purpose;
- an ability to stay removed from family discord;
- an ability to look after oneself;
- high self-esteem;
- an ability to form close personal relationships;
- a positive outlook;
- focused nurturing (i.e. a supportive home life);
- a well-structured household;
- high but achievable expectations from parents.

In addition, grief specialists advise participation in the funeral rites.[9] Genghis would have seen his father's body placed in a seated position, with offerings of meat and *airag*, or fermented mare's milk, followed by a burial, perhaps with a *ger*, a favourite horse, a saddle, a bridle and other luxury items. Possibly his father, as an aristocrat, would have been further honoured with the ritual recorded by a thirteenth-century Chinese official, Peng Daya, who visited Mongolia shortly after Genghis's death: 'Their graves have no mound. Horses are made to trot over them and make them level with the earth.'

Young Genghis had all these factors going for him, as boys raised in the countryside do today. The conditions are rough, the demands high, the training superb, the community close-knit and the self-sufficiency remarkable. Genghis lost one prop – an extended family network – but still had his mother as his anchor. Cast out by her clan, with no animals, she became a gatherer, grubbing for fruits and roots, as *The Secret History* describes:

[9] Worden, *Children and Grief*.[1]

*Born brave, the noble mother*
*Nourished her sons who were favoured*
*With Heaven's good fortune . . .*
*The hungry, nagging sons*
*Who were fed on wild leek*
*And on wild onion by the beautiful lady,*
*Became handsome and good.*

In traditional Mongol society women were chattels, to be given – or stolen – in marriage, yet might also win respect as equals in wisdom, even superiors. Hoelun was a case in point. She makes a terrific role model – impoverished but self-sufficient, determined and strong. Her boys followed her example, fishing and hunting for small animals to help feed the family. Genghis owed his survival to her, and grew strong in mind as well as body. Here is Kets de Vries again, after quoting Richard Branson and Bill Clinton as leaders whose powerful mothers adored and had supreme confidence in their sons: 'It seems to me there is a lot of truth in Freud's famous statement that there is nothing as conducive to success as being your mother's favourite.' A wider community was lost, a smaller, more intensive one gained.

Genghis also gained another asset, a friendship with a boy of his own age named Jamukha. The two ten-year-olds swore an oath, becoming *anda* or 'sworn friends', equivalent to blood-brothers, exchanging dice made of roebuck knucklebone and copper, and playing with them on the frozen River Onon. Next spring they swore friendship again, exchanging arrowheads for hunting – a whistling one from Jamukha, a knob-headed one from Temüjin. No one knows exactly what was involved in taking the *anda* oath, but it meant more than friendship: it was also a bond between tribal chiefs, a political alliance outside the normal ties of kinship.

> They said to each other, 'Listening to the pronouncement of the old men of former ages which says:

>> 'Sworn friends – the two of them
>> 'Share but a single life;
>> 'They do not abandon one another;
>> 'They are each a life's safeguard for the other.'

> We learn that such is the rule by which sworn friends love each other.

## The mental strength to survive

Some years ago I became interested in survivors, particularly in the question of why some survived well and others didn't. At the time, there was a good deal of research into post-traumatic stress disorder. But not all survivors suffered from it. Some seemed better able to cope than others. Likewise, some seemed better suited to staying alive when others died. Why? I acted as interviewer for a TV series, and later made eighteen BBC radio programmes gathering evidence I hoped would answer this question. I heard some remarkable stories, but never came up with the generalizations I had hoped for. I did, however, notice a few obvious pointers: it helps to be familiar with the environment you suddenly find yourself dumped in, or you are likely to succumb to panic and wrong decisions; it's good to have a long-term goal to lift the spirit beyond the immediate threat; it's best not to trust that God is going to help you, because every minute that passes suggests he won't. Less obvious is a paradox: it is helpful to accept the probability of death, yet also fight for life, to combine realism with optimism, to say 'OK, I'm going to die—' with a crucial rider '—but not yet.'[10]

One other generalization seemed to stand the test of many interviews. Most of my survivors had had childhoods that, if not always conventionally happy, had given them a sense of security. It seemed to me that this gave them the most powerful foundation anyone can have to avoid giving up on life: a belief that the universe is fundamentally a supportive place, that it rewards action, and that any setback is a challenge to be overcome. Insecurity in early childhood can act like acid, eating away at this foundation, destroying the very basis of survival, simply because a setback becomes a symbol of a malevolent universe that will get you in the end, undermining your will to fight. It is as if the unconscious mind whispers, 'You always knew the universe had it in for you. You might as well give up.' Security – whether provided by parents, or a wider family, or a group, or a class system, or sometimes a school – gives the healthy child a foundation from which to fight back, to move away from dependence towards independence, and then, if the personality meshes with opportunity, on to the self-confidence from which leadership may spring.[11]

[10] I was unaware of the book currently being written by Al Siebert, *The Survivor Personality*.

[11] There is also a genetic component in resilience, which may be undermined by the so-called 'depression gene'. This gene (a variant of 5-HTT) is triggered by stress and predisposes the bearer to depression by interfering with the production of the neurotransmitter serotonin. Perhaps the gene has been rendered less active by the evolutionary pressure of unforgiving circumstances, like those of traditional Mongolian society, in which depression surely increased the likelihood of death. Now there's an interesting research project.

As he grew into adolescence, Genghis was down, but not at all out, and well equipped to fight back. His parents must have told him all about the time when the clans were briefly unified by his great-grandfather Kabul, at peace with each other, and able to stand against other grassland tribes and the Chinese. He would have heard the story of how Kabul's heir Ambakai had been seized by the Jin and crucified on some sort of a frame known as a 'wooden donkey'. He had died crying for vengeance:

*Until your ten fingers are worn away,*
*Strive to revenge me!*

So Genghis already had the inspiration; he also had the emotional basis for ambition; what he did not have yet was an ability to control himself in a crisis.

One autumn, when he was thirteen, he and his younger half-brother Begter quarrelled over some small items of prey, perhaps because Begter was unwilling to share his catch with his starving step-family, and perhaps as well over who was to be boss of this little gang. Genghis and a younger brother, Khasar, complained to their mother, who reprimanded them:

> 'Why be so malicious? Why do you, older brothers and younger brothers, behave in this way to each other? Just when
>> *'We have no friend but our shadow,*
>> *'We have no whip but our horse's tail.'*

The two boys stormed out in fury. Armed with their bows and arrows, Genghis and Khasar ambushed Begter, and shot him dead.

Hoelun was as distraught as if Begter had been her own son. In words emphasized in verse by *The Secret History*, she gave them a withering dressing-down: 'You who have destroyed life!' she yelled, and tore into them, comparing them to a dozen different aggressive animals. How could they do this, just when – the stock phrase is repeated – we have no friend but our shadow, no whip but our horse's tail?

> *Thus she spoke and*
> *Citing old sayings*
> *Quoting ancient words*
> *She mightily reviled her sons.*

Genghis never forgot this rebuke from the person he respected most in the world, and he remained in awe of his mother for the rest of his life.

Why does *The Secret History* include this hot-headed and cowardly act, with its humiliating put-down? Almost certainly because it was sanctioned by Genghis himself, as all *The Secret History*'s stories must have been. It was a message from the mature Genghis about the immature one, revealing how much this headstrong boy had to learn. One lesson was the need for empathy. His mother's re-action told him, in effect: Remember how you felt when your father died, the shock, the sense of betrayal at his absence? Well, imagine what it is like for the younger, weaker links in your family network when you, the eldest, who should be the most responsible, threaten the family out of anger and short-sightedness!

There's another lesson in all this, one that could not have been consciously recognized until recently.

## GENGHIS'S LEADERSHIP SECRET NO. 2

# ACCEPT CRITICISM

Killing his half-brother was a crime. His mother's anger taught him a lesson he never forgot. A different boy might have become bitter and vindictive. Not Genghis. To be able to accept her rebuke, to allow others to tell the story, was the beginning of a journey towards a character always open to advice and criticism – a prime component in the range of traits known now as emotional intelligence, crucial to leadership at its best.

Psychologists today agree that one element in a repressed personality, in parent or child, is a talent for avoiding confrontation. We all know stock phrases of avoidance: let it go, she'll grow out of it; arguments give me a headache; if you loved me, you wouldn't talk to me that way. But a child who acts destructively, whether physically or socially, *should* be told, and not just for the sake of the household; he or she needs to know – may well be indirectly demanding to know – the boundaries between good and bad behaviour. How otherwise can a child discover the rules of society? How else can it truly be accepted as a member of that society? A parent who constantly placates and avoids confrontation may well be contributing to long-term dysfunctionality in family relationships, leaving a child confused, perhaps even locked into behaviour that will continue on into adulthood. Hoelun did not make that mistake. Here an evil act is directly confronted, in an emotionally secure context. Far from being rejected, the boy is embraced. Far from repressing, he takes it all on board, and then, when grown up – as the existence of this anecdote in *The Secret History* reveals – he wants his people to absorb his experience: the crime, its potentially disastrous consequences and the resolution.

## Two talents: spotting allies and taking decisive action

Genghis, already a boy well able to look after himself, was to face more trials to hone his emerging qualities. The following spring, news of the family's survival reached the Taychiut chief, the one who had abandoned Hoelun and the children. The Taychiuts launched a raid, hunted Genghis down and led him away, a captive.

The story of this episode is powerfully told in *The Secret History*, because it contains a number of insights about Genghis's character. He himself must have encouraged its retelling as propaganda for the cause: this was a leader in the making, with Heaven-sent good fortune.

*This was a leader in the making, with Heaven-sent good fortune.*

For a week or two Genghis was held prisoner, being forced to wear a cangue, a heavy wooden collar locked round his neck and wrists, with a rope attached, which was used to lead and tie the captive.

One night Genghis found himself billeted with a man named Sorkan-shira, an unwilling member of one of the Taychiuts' subject clans. He allowed his two sons to loosen Genghis's cangue to let him sleep more comfortably. Here was a tiny foundation for friendship, should the occasion arise.

The next night was a full moon: Red Circle Day, as the Mongols call the sixteenth day of the first (lunar) month of summer, our May. The tribe gathered for a celebration. *Gers* dotted a broad river valley below slopes with scattered trees, herds grazed between patches of snow, horses stood tethered outside each tent. Among the gathering crowds that afternoon was the captive Genghis, in his cangue, guarded by a 'weakling'.

As darkness fell and the moon rose, the people – many of them the worse for drink – made for their tents. Genghis seized his chance. He jerked the rope out of his custodian's fingers, swung the cangue, hit the guard on the head and ran off into the woods. Behind him he heard a cry – 'I let the prisoner escape!' He had to find somewhere to hide, for he would be easy to see in the moonlight. There was the River Onon. He found a backwater and lay down, head held clear of the icy water by the wooden cangue.

His pursuers searched the woods, but one was on his way home downriver. It was Sorkan-shira. He saw Genghis. Astonished, he muttered that Genghis's Taychiut kinsmen were jealous of him because he had 'fire in his eyes and light in his face'. Then he said, 'Lie just so; I shall not tell them.' Genghis should wait until the coast was clear, then go off to his mother's.

But he couldn't do that. He was trapped in the heavy cangue, which rubbed his neck and wrists raw. He could not ride even if he had a horse. To flee on foot would make him obvious. His clothes were sodden, and the night air was freezing: if he just ran off, he might well die from exposure. So when silence fell, he hauled himself clear of the water and tottered downstream, looking for Sorkan-shira's tent.

He found it, and entered. Sorkan-shira was horrified at the danger, and could hardly wait for Genghis to be gone. His family, though, were as sympathetic as before. The two boys untied the cangue and burned it, put Genghis's clothes to dry, fed him, and hid him outside in a cart of sheep's wool for the rest of the night, all the while telling their younger sister what terrible things they would do if she uttered a sound.

The next day the Taychiuts, continuing their hunt, came to Sorkan-shira's *ger*. They looked everywhere inside, then turned to the cart, with its pile of wool, and were on the point of finding the fugitive when Sorkan-shira could stand it no longer.

'In such heat,' he said, 'how could one stand it amidst the wool?'

Feeling foolish, the searchers left.

Sorkan-shira heaved a sigh of relief. 'You nearly had me blown to the wind like hearth-ashes,' he said, and told Genghis to leave. He stocked him up with food and drink, and gave him a horse and a bow with two arrows; but no saddle or tinder which could be traced back to those who had harboured him. Genghis rode away upstream, and finally rejoined his family.

In all this, his instinct for survival served him well. He kept his nerve, took decisive action at the right moment, and made a good choice of ally. Revenge would be sweet, but only if it did not compromise security. To achieve both, he needed more than bravery, more than a warrior's skills. He needed the social and political skills of the true leader. By the time he was fifteen, those skills were well founded.

# First steps in diplomacy

And he had a foundation on which to build. Years previously, just before he was killed, Genghis's father had taken him to a distant *ger* belonging to a member of a clan from which Genghis's people traditionally chose wives. The two children, though only about nine or ten, were engaged. Now sixteen, Genghis returned to marry his betrothed, Börte.

*The Secret History* does not describe the wedding, because everyone would have known the rituals involved and it would have added nothing to our knowledge of his character. The only thing of significance is a gift for Genghis's mother, a winter coat of black sable. It must have been a magnificent object: long and luxurious, jet-black and oil-smooth. Genghis and his brothers at once spotted the coat's value and set it aside for safe-keeping – presumably with Hoelun's consent; would they have dared otherwise?

Genghis lost no time in consolidating his increased status as a married eldest son. He had a right-hand man, named Boorchu, who had helped him recover some stolen horses. He could already count on his own brothers and surviving half-brother, on Jamukha, and on the clan from which both his mother and his wife came. He could do with more help, though; and he knew where to look for it.

Long before Genghis had been born, his father Yisügei had allied himself with the greatest tribal leader north of the Great Wall. Toghril, chief of the Kereyids, had killed several uncles to secure the throne, and been forced to flee by a vengeful relative. Yisügei had helped him regain the leadership. The two had become 'sworn friends', the strongest bond between unrelated men. Now Toghril, having broken down the clan system that had previously kept the Kereyids at each other's throats, commanded two 'ten-thousands', two divisions, with an elite force of bodyguards. To win him over was Genghis's first political challenge. The connection with his father was enough to get Genghis a hearing, but not enough to win commitment. But he did have something persuasive to offer: the black sable coat. It worked. 'In return for the black sable coat,' Toghril said, 'I shall bring together for you your divided people.'

Warren Bennis, professor and founding chairman of the University of California's Leadership Institute, writes of this precarious moment in a young leader's career in a witty article based on Jaques' 'Seven Ages of Man' speech in *As You Like It*. The 'mewling and puking' infant is the pre-leader, who needs a parent figure, a mentor, to help in making the first decisions. (Mentor, by the way, was the friend in whose hands Odysseus placed his affairs when he left for the Trojan War, in particular the care of his son Telemachus; it's from Mentor's name that we take our word for a trusted guide.) It is a sign of early maturity that an ambitious young man or woman can recognize the need for guidance, and seek

*It is a sign of early maturity that an ambitious young man or woman can recognize the need for guidance, and seek out a mentor.*

out a mentor, or accept one with good grace. Genghis's mentor and father-figure was the wily, experienced Toghril

– who would, however, prove unreliable, forcing Genghis further along the path of self-reliance.

# A vision to inspire himself, and win followers

Around 1181, when Genghis was about 19, came another reverse. News of his rise had reached the Merkits, a tribe of many clans living to the north on the Selenge river, just over the border that divides present-day Russia and Mongolia. Genghis's mother, Hoelun, had been stolen from them by his father, and they bore a grudge. It would demand a large-scale operation to launch a raid across 350 kilometres of forest, river and open grassland, but now was a good time to take revenge, before Genghis became too powerful.

Early one morning, when Genghis's family were camping in a broad valley near the headwaters of the Kherlen, an old servant-woman woke to the sound of galloping hooves and shouted a warning. Hoelun picked up her five-year-old daughter and joined the young men fleeing upriver into the forests of Burkhan Khaldun, while Börte and the elderly servant, left without mounts, took an enclosed ox-drawn carriage, and were soon overtaken. Young men dismounted, opened the door, and saw their prize. An extensive search on Burkhan Khaldun's forbidding flanks came to nothing. They withdrew with their captive.

Now came Genghis's flight into the forests of Burkhan Khaldun, his three days of hiding, his miraculous escape, his thank-offering to the sacred mountain and to Heaven, and in due course the conviction, in his own mind and in the minds of his followers, that he was protected by Heaven.

Nowadays no one would believe that this idea could have really come from Heaven, literally out of the blue. Once, though, in less sceptical times, it was commonplace for kings and emperors to claim divine backing and be taken seriously. In the Christian and Jewish West, the notion, rooted in the Pentateuch, was an article of faith for millennia. Kings always liked to get divine sanction through the Church whenever possible, which was why, for example, Charlemagne arranged for the pope to crown him Holy Roman Emperor in AD 800. In the early seventeenth century James I formalized the principle, writing that a king was 'ordained for his people, having received from God a burden of government'. Fossil phrases and letters preserve the idea: British coins still state that the Queen holds her position 'DG' – 'Dei Gratia', by the grace of God. The East believed it as well, with Chinese emperors claiming the Mandate of Heaven when they inherited or seized power. But a valid claim depended on more than power: the claimant needed to preserve unity, perform the right rituals and show moral stature. Genghis's forefathers, perhaps Genghis himself, knew this, for they had been in touch with the Jin dynasty, which had claimed the Mandate when it took over in north-east China in 1125. Genghis and his family also knew of Toghril's faith, Nestorian Christianity. Perhaps he too claimed a God-given right to rule. In any event, any leader worth his salt needed divine backing. What's interesting about *The Secret History*'s version of events is that it backdates the claim, Heaven having preordained Genghis *before* he rose to power, whereas in the Chinese view Heaven's support came *after* accession.

This is an important step towards leadership. There had

been many armies, conquests and invasions, but not many inspired by an ideology rooted in spirituality. There is no hint that Toghril, though he was a Nestorian Christian, fought his battles in the name of Christ, for Christ's message was, on the whole, one of peace. But over on the other side of Asia had arisen a creed that linked spirituality and war: Islam. Although the Prophet taught that 'there shall be no coercion in matters of faith', and although the Quran sanctions only 'just' wars of defence, Islam's followers quickly mixed sectarian strife and political strife, and the faith spread with the sword. Its destiny was to bring the whole world into 'submission' (which is what 'Islam' means). The Mongols were in contact with Muslim traders. Is it just an odd coincidence that the idea of divine support and of world rule should have come to a young Mongol ambitious for power and political unity? I think not, though there is not a shred of evidence to back me up.

Genghis was now on the brink of stepping up to the next level of leadership. First had come an education in survival; then growing self-sufficiency; then a willingness to seek and take on responsibility. And now clan leadership, with its round of vital but routine decisions about when and where to pasture, hunt and camp. But perhaps he already had something greater in mind. He would have remembered his father's tales of what Kabul had achieved, of the call to revenge the crucified Ambakai. He would have inherited his father's ambitions to achieve wider power. Perhaps his closest companions were beginning to take his wild words about divine protection seriously. As an ambitious elder son, surely he would have wished not simply to match his father and his forefather Kabul, but to excel them both.

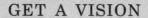

## GET A VISION

Leaders and leadership theorists talk a good deal about the need for vision. But an inspiring vision is a rare combination of the right circumstances, the right vision and the right person, who must dream it up, communicate it and get followers to believe in it. Genghis's vision of tribal unity at first threatened his rivals. So unity alone was not enough. He could simply have seemed overweening. It was the combination of initial success and his belief in divine backing that inspired loyalty in would-be rivals. Then the vision could grow: Mongols could rule a nation, an empire, the world.

In what follows, watch for clues to Genghis's agenda. He is determined to build security for himself and his people. That means an escape, at last, from the endless round of fratricidal squabbles, blood-feuds and revenge-takings. That in its turn means an end to traditional tribalism. How on earth is that to be achieved? Only by dissolving the tribes themselves, by making all their members honorary Mongols. It is not mere destruction he is after, but destruction for a purpose, with an agenda suggested by the events that now unfold.

# 2

# WARLORD:
# HOW TO MAKE
# A NATION

G ENGHIS'S NEXT task involved his first recorded act of leadership: he had to rescue Börte, or see his reputation damaged beyond repair. That almost happened anyway, because, as a would-be leader, he got off to a shaky start.

He turned to the man he called 'father', Toghril, who was as good as his word. The older man promised two cavalry divisions, and told Genghis to call on his childhood friend Jamukha, now head of his own clan, and as much of a man to be reckoned with as Genghis. Messengers galloped back and forth between the three leaders: Toghril on the grasslands near present-day Ulaanbaatar, Genghis 250 kilometres away near the Khenti mountains, Jamukha another 100 kilometres beyond on the banks of the River Onon. Linking them was no easy matter. The 700-kilometre round trip would have taken a week or so, with many changes of horse. Jamukha undertook to provide another division, and gave detailed instructions about when to meet, and where – in the northern part of the tangle of mountains and valleys that formed the Mongol heartland.

The Secret History gives a detailed account of what followed, providing another lesson in the fundamentals of leadership in twelfth-century Mongolia. Toghril's forces rolled eastward, gathering Genghis's much smaller group, then swung north around the Khenti mountains to meet Jamukha.

But something went wrong. Jamukha, with only about 100 kilometres to travel, had already been in place for three days, and he was becoming increasingly angry. This was not open steppe but pastureland, hemmed in by mountains and forests. Here were several thousand men, eating into their own food supplies, increasingly restless to get back to their herds, with two or three spare mounts each, grazing over several thousand hectares. Moreover, any wandering Merkit could easily have spotted the army and galloped off with a warning. Every day's delay threatened disaster. These were lessons that *The Secret History* emphasized by setting Jamukha's fury to verse:

> *Did we not agree that we won't be late*
> *At the appointed meeting,*
> *Even if there be a blizzard;*
> *At the gathering*
> *Even if there be rain?*

Are we not Mongols, for whom a 'yes' is the same as being bound by an oath?

Genghis and Toghril took the criticism without complaint, the elder man acknowledging: 'As we are three days late at the meeting place, it is up to younger brother Jamukha to punish and lay blame!' And it is for the future leader of the nation – and the nation's elite, listening to the story – to take note: whatever happens, if you as leader make a promise, *you keep your word*. That was one lesson

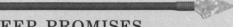

*Whatever happens,
if you as leader
make a promise,
you keep your
word.*

Genghis learned from this
experience, and from his
sworn friend, who was,
thankfully, able to criticize
and yet still remain com-
mitted to the purpose of the
campaign. There is a second
lesson implicit in the story:
Toghril, 'father' to young
Genghis, has the wisdom to accept justified criticism. If
there is a truth to be revealed, leaders should be open to
receive it. In this case, things might have turned out very
differently: an insecure leader taking offence, withdraw-
ing, sinking into resentment, rivalry and finally outright
violence. As it was, the three renewed their alliance, and
moved on.

For a week or so, the four divisions – 12,000 men or
more – worked their way north over the mountains for
almost 400 kilometres to the Merkit camp. The operation

was too huge to achieve total surprise. Warned by hunts-men, the Merkit fled in panic, sweeping along their prized hostage Börte in one of the fleeing carts. Among the pursuers was Genghis, calling for her. She heard, jumped down, came running through the darkness, seized his bridle, and 'they fell into each other's arms'. It makes a romantic picture – surely too romantic to be true – but it underscores the success of the campaign. The Merkits were scattered, many of the women taken as concubines and servants; Börte was saved; and Genghis, the wiser for his error, was now a true leader, admired as a provider of booty and women who was willing to risk all for love, honour and revenge.

One shadow remained. Börte had not only been seized and kept by the Merkits for months; she had been raped. When Genghis found her, she was pregnant with her eldest child, a boy named Jochi. No one could tell if this was Genghis's child or a 'Merkit bastard', as one of Genghis's other boys called him later. No matter. If Genghis minded, he did not show it, either to Börte or to his people. Doubts about paternity were common enough in a culture in which women were often kidnapped and rescued. Jochi would turn out to have his faults – he was a boaster, and often too eager to counter his father's will – but Genghis always treated him as a true son.

## The risks and rewards of treachery

For eighteen months Genghis's family lived with Jamukha's, at first in harmony, then with increasing tension. One or the other had to become dominant. As *The Secret History* puts it, the rivalry comes into the open when Jamukha presents Genghis with a choice: should they camp near a mountain, where the herders could find good shelter? Or by a river, where the lambs would get good food? Genghis is puzzled. He goes to ask his mother for advice, but Börte butts in. Jamukha gets tired of people, she says. Now he's tired of us. He could be hatching some sort of a plot, or forcing a crisis in leadership. We should separate. Let's move on.

And so they do.

Scholars have been as puzzled as Genghis by this passage. Why is he puzzled? Perhaps because he is the junior partner, yet Jamukha, the boss, does not take this routine decision himself. But then, why this odd business of Hoelun being interrupted by Börte?

Igor de Rachewiltz, in his commentary on the translation of *The Secret History*, suggests an answer. The passage, which sets up a split in the tribe, was written to shift the blame for the decision on to Jamukha and Börte. Genghis comes out as (a) the poor, puzzled victim for whom we have sympathy, who has (b) respect for his mother and (c) the good sense to listen to his wife. In fact, the truth is that Genghis has decided to make his bid for leadership by forcing a choice upon the Mongol clan leaders. The version we have, therefore, is in de Rachewiltz's words the 'official' justification for what was, in effect, Genghis's 'callous betrayal of his sworn friend and ally'. Well, perhaps. If so, it was not the first time – nor would it be the last – that a would-be leader turned on a friend to fulfil his ambition, and then used the media to shift the blame on to the victim.

Genghis might have simply marched away into isolation and obscurity. But the opposite happened. *The*

*Secret History* condenses a process of small-scale conquests and capitulations into a tight-knit drama. At dawn, other clans join Genghis: first three, then another five, then more, all choosing Genghis as leader rather than Jamukha, for Genghis offers something Jamukha does not: commitment, loyalty, generosity (and also, if de Rachewiltz is right, the threat of ruthless animosity towards his enemies). Rumour spreads that young Genghis is the one the Mongols need to restore their lost unity, and security, and wealth. *The Secret History* resorts to blatant propaganda, telling of a flatterer named Khorchi who arrives with news of a timely vision:

> A heavenly sign appeared before my very eyes, revealing the future to me . . . A hornless and fallow ox lifted up the great shaft under the tent, harnessed it on to himself and pulled it after him. As he proceeded following Genghis on the wide road, he kept bellowing: 'Together Heaven and Earth have agreed: Genghis shall be the lord of the people!'

So it goes: signs and portents and defections and oaths from clan chiefs jostling to be stewards, animal-tenders, managers of cart-tents and sword-carriers.

To see how Genghis emerged on top would be to enter into a complex game, played out on shifty ground – if we had the details. Tradition dictated that leaders did not lightly discard the bonds of family, clan and sworn brother-hood; but discarded they often were, given a powerful enough reason to do so, and to endure the attendant heartache. In the early 1190s Genghis was still at best

No. 2, and at several points very nearly something much less. Yet he came through. How is not always clear, for much is obscure in *The Secret History*. It's fair to guess that the full story would have been well known, and that Genghis's advantage lay in his skill at balancing diplomacy with treachery. *The Secret History* makes sure he emerges with his good side intact by suppressing the bad.

Once, for instance, Jamukha sent a force to attack Genghis. The result was catastrophic for Genghis, who fled to the rugged upper reaches of the Onon, protected again by the foothills of Burkhan Khaldun. In *The Secret History*'s somewhat incoherent account of these events, one startling incident stands out. Jamukha had 'the princes of the Chinos [Wolves] boiled alive in 70 cauldrons'. Scholars have argued for years about what this means. Most assume that it refers to the male leaders of a small clan loyal to Genghis, whose legendary totemic forefather had been a wolf, or a leader of that name. Boiling alive was indeed an established form of execution, though it is fair to assume that 70 is not an exact number and simply means 'many'. In addition, Jamukha cut off the head of an enemy chief and dragged it away tied to his horse's tail. These two examples of deliberate brutality and humiliation are set in implied contrast to Genghis's style of leadership. If Jamukha, even in victory, is a brutal murderer eager to rule by terror, then Genghis, even in defeat, is the opposite.

But there is another lesson hidden here. Later, Genghis, as national leader, would be a master of terror, unleashing death and destruction in truly horrific ways. So what, one may ask, is wrong with Jamukha's boiling 70 opponents alive and dragging a severed head about behind a horse? What's wrong is that it doesn't work. Genghis and his gang are not cast down, do not surrender. Just the opposite. The atrocity spurs him to greater efforts to achieve vengeance and victory. Jamukha's action is that of a poor leader, not because he perpetrates an atrocity, but because he perpetrates *the wrong sort of atrocity*. If extreme violence is going to be useful, it has to be well chosen, and done not out of passion but out of cold calculation. Terror has to weigh advantages and disadvantages, and balance them in your favour. It has to save lives on your own side. It has to serve your own interests. Like a kung-fu master, the leader must either opt for magnanimity, in order to work with former enemies, or commit to total ruthlessness. As the United States discovered in Vietnam and Iraq, half and half – good intentions on the one hand and appalling behaviour on the other – does not work; nor, as Germany's Blitz on London revealed, does a half-hearted atrocity: both harden resistance. It may have been this episode that taught Genghis a lesson he would apply with appalling effectiveness in China and the Islamic world.

On another occasion, news came that Jin (north China) had sent a force to attack the Tatars, the tribe on the borderlands of Jin and Mongolia. They had been cultivated by Jin, bribed and cajoled to act as buffers between Jin and the Mongols. But nothing was stable, with Mongols, other tribes and Tatars constantly realigning themselves to fight with or against the Jin and each other. At this moment, the Jin had lost patience with their erstwhile vassals and sent an army to bring them into line. Genghis took an instant decision: he summoned Toghril to take advantage of this golden opportunity to attack the people who had poisoned his father, the man who had been Toghril's sworn friend. The two joined up, mounted their own attack on the Tatars, and won – thus driving the Tatars to support Jamukha.

Why did he do this? Not simply to destroy old enemies, which it failed to do anyway. It opened up a relationship with Jin, the great power to the south. That was where wealth lay. The Jin capital was Beijing, a place of art and poetry and fine foods and silks, with academies for Chinese and Jurchen officials, and examination systems in the Chinese style. No wonder Genghis was keen to ally himself with Jin. It worked, too. The local commander made him a *quri*. No one knows what *quri* meant, so it could not have been a high honour, but it was at least an entrée into a world of wealth and sophistication, if he ever chose to make use of it.

Among the Mongols themselves, still split among half a dozen squabbling factions, there was still much to be decided. At some point, there was a great battle on the plains of eastern Mongolia, during which Jamukha's coalition with the Tatars was overwhelmed by a terrible storm and fell apart. Jamukha himself escaped, but the Tatars were doomed. Genghis promised:

*We shall measure the Tatars against the linchpin of a cart*
*And kill them to the last one.*

This sounds like genocide, sparing only the children small enough to fit under a cart-axle. In fact, it was a good deal less atrocious than it sounds, since it referred only to the adult and teenage males of the leading families: 'The rest we shall enslave.' Remember (a) that the Tatars had killed Genghis's father; (b) that the tribes were traditional enemies; (c) that it might have been the other way around; and (d) that this dire act worked. The Tatars were finished as a force: the survivors were turned into assets, and took on new identities as Mongols. Two aristocratic Tatar women were taken by Genghis as wives, one of whom, Yisui, became as close to him as his senior wife Börte. A little boy, Shigi, was adopted into Genghis's family, later rising to high office as chief judge.

If *The Secret History* skimps on politics, strategy and military details, its author was at pains to record examples of the one trait that Genghis valued above all – loyalty, the most fundamental of virtues in life on the steppe. In a battle, Genghis is wounded by an arrow. One man risks his life to save Genghis's, sucking poisoned blood from his wound, then creeping into the enemy camp to steal food; another – a prisoner – owns up to firing an arrow that killed Genghis's horse. In both cases, bravery and honesty are rewarded, and both men went on to become generals.

*Loyalty was the most fundamental of virtues in life on the steppe.*

But personal loyalty – theirs to Genghis, his to them – is not the essence of this virtue. After the battle, the Taychiut chief who had held Genghis captive was himself captured by a man of a subordinate clan and his two sons. This chief, Kiriltuk, was so overweight he could not ride a horse, for which he had been nicknamed Targutai ('Fatty'). The three forced 'Fatty' Kiriltuk into a cart, and set off to surrender with their prize. On the way, however, they remembered Genghis's uncompromising views on loyalty, and began to doubt the wisdom of their actions. Their captive was, after all, the chief to whom they had sworn allegiance. Wouldn't Genghis say, 'People who lay hands on their rightful lord should be cut down'? Rather than reveal themselves to Genghis as traitors, they let their captive go, and presented themselves to Genghis empty-handed. Wise move. Even though Genghis would have executed Kiriltuk, he placed loyalty above vengeance.

It is not loyalty to a particular lord and master that Genghis upholds, then; it is loyalty to the very idea of loyalty. This, it seems to me, is a remarkable advance in his leadership: acknowledgement that the *role* of leader is of more significance than the person of the leader. In European monarchies, especially in times of civil strife, aristocrats agonized about where their loyalty should lie: with the crown, or the person who wore it; with the idea or the individual? In China, officials went through similar agonies when Heaven seemed to be transferring its Mandate to a new dynasty: at what moment, precisely, should one switch loyalties? It is this thought that, in mature democracies, lies behind loyalty to the idea of democracy: you win, you lose, leaders come and go, but whatever happens, as government or 'loyal opposition', you uphold the ideal accepted by leaders and followers alike.

Here was something that Genghis accepted and promoted as a 'core value' that underpinned his leadership. As Goleman comments, such leaders 'exude resonance: They have genuine passion for their mission, and that passion is contagious.'

## To the brink of defeat

Battle followed battle, victories and defeats balanced each other, until at one low point Genghis had to flee to survive. Down to a mere 2,600 men, he pulled away, along the Khalkha river, and then to the shores of a lake called Baljuna, though where it was has never been agreed. What followed assumed huge significance, because it marked not only Genghis's nadir in military terms, but also a turning point in terms of leadership. The future emperor was again close to extinction, as recorded in Chinese sources. According to these, Genghis endured extreme deprivation with nineteen loyal companions (each of whom had his own demoralized contingents). They were a mixed bunch of Mongols, Muslims, Uighurs and Khitans, united by Genghis and his broad, non-racist vision. All were reduced to drinking the muddy waters of Lake Baljuna.

In the words of one of two almost identical accounts:

> Upon arrival at the Baljuna, the provisions were used up. It happened that from the north a wild horse ran up. [Jochi] Khasar brought it down. From its skin they made a kettle; with a stone they got fire, and from the river, water. They boiled the flesh of the horse and ate it. Genghis Khan, raising his hand toward the sky, swore thus: 'If I finish "the great work" [the founding of a united nation], then I shall share with you men the sweet and the bitter; if I break my word, then let me be as this water.'

This was the moment at which a leader willing to share suffering, defeat and death with his companions forges a bond like no other. Shakespeare knew the importance of sharing suffering, risking all, when he has the future Henry V, before fighting the French at Agincourt, say:

*For he today that sheds his blood with me*
*Shall be my brother.*

The experience of 'drinking the muddy waters' was Genghis's St Crispian's Day. Those who were part of the Baljuna Covenant, as scholars call it, became a band of brothers who would glory in their shared hardship and the bonds between lord, commanders and warriors. This was a story that 'good men told their sons'. (Well, not all of them. Despite its significance, the incident was totally omitted from *The Secret History*, probably because by the time it was written some of the companions had become *personae non gratae*.)

Many other leaders have known how to inspire by setting present suffering against a noble cause. Witness Churchill on 13 May 1940, after just three days as prime minister, and three days after the German invasion of Belgium and Holland. France would soon fall. Britain would stand alone. He told his Cabinet: 'I have nothing to offer but blood, toil, tears and sweat.' He repeated that phrase later in the day when he asked the House of Commons for a vote of confidence in his new all-party government, and added grim, inspiring words – inspiring because of their grimness:

We have before us an ordeal of the most grievous kind. We have before us many, many long months of struggle and of suffering. You ask, what is our

GENGHIS'S LEADERSHIP SECRET NO. 5

## SHARE HARDSHIP

Genghis's vision was revolutionary: an end to tribalism, national unity. The nature of revolutionary leadership demands sacrifice. In the words of James MacGregor Burns, 'The leaders must be absolutely dedicated to the cause and able to demonstrate that commitment by giving time and effort to it, risking their lives, undergoing imprisonment, exile, persecution and continual hardship.' Sharing suffering does not guarantee success, and many a brave, misguided leader died in vain, forgotten; but a refusal to do so is an almost certain guarantee of failure. Genghis was in good company. Those successful revolutionary leaders who suffered for their cause and followers include Alexander, Jesus, Mohammed, Mao, Lenin, Castro and Mandela.

policy? I can say: It is to wage war, by sea, land and air, with all our might and with all the strength that God can give us; to wage war against a monstrous tyranny, never surpassed in the dark, lamentable catalogue of human crime. That is our policy. You ask, what is our aim? I can answer in one word: It is victory, victory at all costs, victory in spite of all terror, victory, however long and hard the road may be.

Someone else who gave the matter of reviving morale much thought was General Sir William Slim, who in 1943 was faced with restoring the morale of Britain's 14th Army after the Japanese drove it out of Burma into India. As he explains in his book *Defeat into Victory*, 'morale is a state of mind', which must be created on three levels: spiritual, intellectual and material. By 'spiritual' morale he meant not religious fervour, but belief in a great and noble cause, that must be pursued at once with aggression, by every man, each of whom must feel his actions have a direct bearing on the outcome. Intellectually, he must feel that the object is attainable, that his group is efficient and that his leaders are to be trusted. Finally, all men must feel they are provided for materially, with the tools for the job, in both weapons and conditions. This is virtually a blueprint of what Genghis presented to his commanders at Baljuna, a blueprint for almost every force facing apparently overwhelming odds (not, however, for those few unusual cases in which men see a greater virtue in self-sacrifice than in victory: Japan's kamikaze pilots, today's Muslim suicide bombers).

One other benefit of sharing hardship is that it makes it impossible for leader and followers alike to deny harsh facts. For military commanders and corporate leaders alike, seeing, telling and absorbing the unpleasant truth is an important part of retaining morale, for there is nothing so destructive as optimism that is constantly confounded by events. In his analysis of what makes good companies great, Jim Collins concludes: 'There is a sense of exhilaration that comes in facing head-on the hard truths and saying, "We will never give up. We will never capitulate. It may take a long time, but we *will* find a way to prevail."'

Even when reduced to next to nothing, Genghis managed to keep up morale, by facing the truth, yet remaining committed to a cause which seemed just and great: in the name of Eternal Heaven, victory, leading on to further conquest and unity. And it worked: 'Among the officers and men, there was none who was not moved to tears.'

Luck was with him. His enemies fell, one by one. The Tatars were defeated, their menfolk exterminated, the women and children taken as wives, secondary wives and slaves. Jamukha and Toghril fled westward, into Naiman territory. Toghril was killed by a guard who refused to believe the refugee was the great khan of the Kereyids. The Naimans too were conquered, forcing Jamukha to flee into the mountains of the far north-west with five other survivors, seeking the help of the Merkits, the people who had captured Börte 20 years before. A final campaign ended with the Merkits' renewed defeat. Jamukha was captured, betrayed by his companions. According to *The Secret History*, Genghis, for whom treachery against any lord and master was the ultimate crime, executed Jamukha's companions, then gave Jamukha a chance to recant, calling to mind their old friendship:

> *Let us each remind the other of what he has forgotten,*
> *Let us each wake up the other who has fallen asleep,*
> *Although you separated from me*
> *And went a different way,*
> *You remain my lucky, blessed sworn friend.*

He was offering Jamukha a way out, looking for a way to show mercy. It was Jamukha who condemned himself, in powerful words.

Now that the world is at your disposal, of what use
would I be as a companion to you?  On the contrary,
O my sworn friend,

> *I would intrude into your dreams in the dark night*
> *I would trouble your heart in the bright day*
> *I would be a louse in your collar,*
> *I would be a thorn in the inner lapel of your coat.*

The fault lay in his stars, he says, or, as we would put it, in
adverse circumstances – a common excuse made by failed
leaders. As Jim Collins points out, good leaders ascribe
success to good luck; but they take responsibility for
failures. Not Jamukha, who blamed everything and everyone but himself: 'I lost my parents when I was small, and
had no younger brothers. My wife is a prattler, my companions untrustworthy . . . I was conquered by the august
spirit of my sworn friend who is of higher birth.' Now
there was nothing left but death, and at this point he is
allowed to regain a measure of dignity. 'Let them kill me
without shedding blood . . . When I lie dead, my bones
buried in a high place, for ever and ever I shall protect you,
and be a blessing to the offspring of your offspring . . . Now
do away with me quickly!' Genghis honoured his request,
by having him strangled or his back broken.

This, at least, is *The Secret History*'s well-spun story,
which has the gloss of carefully crafted propaganda. From
it Jamukha emerges as a former hero who strayed into
brutality and treachery, but in the end regains the nobility
that justifies Genghis's earlier trust. And Genghis is
portrayed as the wise and generous leader, who never
breaks the sacred bond of blood-brotherhood and is

ennobled by the words of his victim. I think, if this episode were ever read to Genghis's royal descendants, there would not have been a dry eye in the *ger*.

## Looking towards peace and stability

A new society this big needed new rules to underpin its administration. This challenge produced one of Genghis's most remarkable insights. It sprang from his conception of what national unity would mean. Previously (and also in centuries to come, when the Mongols were once again torn apart by civil war and warlordism), it was enough for a leader to be little more than a robber baron. But for Genghis conquest was a means to an end: ultimately, universal rule. Heaven had, for whatever inexplicable reason, given the world to the Mongols. Their task was to have every other people, nation and culture acknowledge this astonishing fact. Inevitably, therefore, conquest was not a one-off assault by a warlord ending in mayhem and looting, but continuous administration. And administration meant lasting governorship, which would involve records, taxes, collectors, accountants – in a phrase, w*ritten* administration.

*It is a tribute to his leadership qualities that Genghis acknowledged his own inadequacy and sought a solution.*

This was an extraordinary conclusion for a 'barbarian' leader, raised in an oral culture. Until then, histories, myths and traditions would have been stored in human memory. Messages were carried by messengers, usually in verse, which is easier to remember (like those passed between allies and enemies when Genghis was fighting for domination). Now, new laws and new institutions made memory inadequate. Too much was happening, and if it was to last it had to be recorded. It is a tribute to his leadership qualities that Genghis, influenced no doubt by his advisers, acknowledged his own inadequacy and sought a solution.

There were a number of possible choices of writing systems among the Mongols' sophisticated urban neighbours to the south: the highly literate Jin, Tangut and Song cultures (they would also have known of a fourth, Liao, which had preceded the Jin, flourishing from 916 to 1125). There would no doubt have been much discussion in Genghis's royal *gers*. What sort of writing would work best? The non-Chinese empires to the south had based their systems on Chinese script: Liao and Jin had adapted Chinese, the Tanguts had invented a Chinese-looking script of their own. But Chinese and its derivatives are hard, because they are based on word-syllables represented by many thousand symbols, which are strung together to make many more thousand 'words'. For outsiders, mastering such a script is a huge intellectual challenge. Besides, Mongols had always looked down on non-nomadic cultures, and would have been reluctant to accept their scripts even if they had been easy. Far better to use an alphabetical script, with only a few dozen characters, each roughly representing a sound. They would, of course, have known about Tibetan, an alphabetical script that had been in existence for some 500 years. But there was a solution closer to hand, and someone who could apply it.

One of those captured from the Naimans was a scribe named Tatar-Tonga, who had been the Naimans' chief administrator. He was a Uighur, one of a Turkic people who had ruled Mongolia some 400 years earlier and had close links with other Turkic groups in Central Asia, in particular the Sogdian city-states of present-day Uzbekistan. The Uighurs got on well with the Mongols; they would later declare themselves for Genghis voluntarily. They used an ancient script with roots in the original alphabetical systems that emerged from the Middle East in the first millennium BC. Like all alphabetical scripts, Uighur writing could be adapted to any language, as the Roman and Cyrillic systems have been. Tatar-Tonga had used Uighur to keep the Naiman records. The Uighurs, scattered in the mid-ninth century, preserved their culture as traders and moneylenders along the trade routes that linked China to Central Asia and India and the world of Islam. By Genghis's time the script had evolved into a flowing form, written vertically from top to bottom and left to right. This was the script that arrived on Genghis's threshold just when he needed it, lodged in the mind of just the right man. Tatar-Tonga was picked up on the battlefield after the defeat of the Naimans in 1204, clasping the state seal and looking for his sovereign. Impressed by his loyalty, Genghis took the scribe into his service and ordered him to adapt the Uighur script to Mongol, and teach it to the younger princes.

This was a remarkable exercise in objectivity – to be able to identify this need, acknowledge his own inadequacy, see the problem clearly and employ someone smarter than he was to solve it. The response makes for an interesting comparison with another marauder 800 years earlier: Attila the Hun. Attila, too, had forged a barbarian empire, centred on Hungary, on the borders of one of the

## GENGHIS'S LEADERSHIP SECRET NO. 6

# KNOW YOUR OWN LIMITATIONS

Poor leaders hide limitations and lay claim to genius, often with ludicrous results. Mussolini was 'always right'; Idi Amin proclaimed himself Conqueror of the British Empire. Great leaders acknowledge inadequacies, and seek to make them good. Genghis saw that his vision of national unity could not be made to work by applying the current skills of illiterate nomads. He admitted his inadequacy, saw what was needed, and hired someone cleverer than himself – and a non-Mongol, moreover – to solve the problem. The Uighur writing system introduced by Tatar-Tonga, a Uighur employed by the defeated Naimans, was used to write *The Secret History* as well as Genghis's laws. Genghis's insight ensured that the story of his rise survived.

world's greatest and most powerful cultures, Rome. He too succeeded by a combination of ruthlessness and robber-baron violence, raiding Rome's eastern provinces as Genghis raided the Tatars and (later) Jin. He acquired vast wealth, which he used to win over and keep on his side tribes from the Danube to the Baltic, and across southern Russia – an area about half the size of the United States. He, like Genghis, employed foreigners to help with his administration. All this he built up in about ten years, AD 440–50.

At this stage, he could have stopped, and consolidated. He might have traded his way to ever greater wealth, built himself a lasting capital, instead of one of wooden palisades. He might have developed a system of taxation to circulate his wealth, to feed his people, and to provide them with the basics of Roman-style civilization. But he couldn't. He never saw that the one thing his culture lacked was writing. It would not have been hard; his Latin scribes could have recorded Hunnish; perhaps there was in his community of bards a Hunnish *Iliad* telling of Hunnish origins, awaiting a script that never came. All we have of the language is a few names as transcribed into Latin and a few tentative links with Turkish. It was not in Attila's character to admit inadequacies and change tack. As a result he remained a robber-baron, keeping his followers happy with booty. It was an economy that depended on expansion, and ever more expansion, but with no greater purpose, no vision. In consequence he was driven into an almost impossible enterprise – the seizure of Rome's western empire, in two huge campaigns that foundered in defeat and drove him to a drunken death in 453. Had he been different, a Genghis figure, he could have had so much more: all of Gaul, wealth beyond anything he imagined, and immortality. Why, in a different universe all of northern Europe might have ended up speaking and writing Hunnish.

As it was he remained a leader stuck at Level 4, in Jim Collins's terms: egotistical, charismatic, driven by short-term gains, unable to look after his succession. When he died, his empire collapsed into civil war. It was gone in an eye-blink.

# 3

# REFORMER:
# THE FOUNDING
# FATHER

TEMÜJIN WAS now master of all Mongolia's tribes, all 'the people of the felt-walled tents'. In 1206 a national assembly – *khuriltai*, from which *khural*, the modern word for parliament, derives – proclaimed him khan, and invested him with the title Genghis.[1]

Scholars debate the origins of the title. No traditional title, whether Turkish, Mongol or Chinese, would have been right, for no Mongol had risen to such a height. 'Genghis' – Chinggis or Chingis, in its more correct transliterations – was an invented title, never conferred before or since, and its origins are much disputed. A once-popular suggestion was that it derived from the Turkish for 'sea', *tengiz*, the sea being an object of admiration (when in the sixteenth century a later khan wished to honour the highest Buddhist dignitary, he made up a Mongolian version of the lama's Tibetan title and called him the *dalai* lama, using the Mongolian word for 'sea'.) Or perhaps the name was intended to mirror the word for Heaven or Sky, *Tenger*, putting its holder on a par with the

---

[1] Actually, the date of his investiture is not 100 per cent certain. It may have been earlier. But something big happened in 1206, and scholars accept that this was the occasion on which the title was either confirmed or granted.

Chinese emperors who ruled with the 'Mandate of Heaven'. The most recently offered, and most compelling, suggestion is that *chingis*, found in a ninth- or tenth-century inscription in runic script, was a Turkish–Mongol word meaning 'fierce, hard, tough', which made it utterly suitable. The word seems to have become *ching* in old Mongolian, but then dropped out of use.[2]

This was the moment his loyal companions had been working, fighting and waiting for, and Genghis did not disappoint, as *The Secret History* records at length. Those who had stood by him became commanders of 'thousands', of which there were 95 in all – 95,000 men, at most, which with their households suggests a total population of half a million: not many with which to start on world conquest. All those others who had helped him were rewarded with high offices. The names recalled past adventures and foreshadowed future eminence: four generals were called his 'war-horses', four others named as his 'hounds'; this one who had once rescued Genghis's sons, that one whose sons had been excellent spies, those who had shown what loyalty meant by releasing their fat lord Kiriltuk. Sorkan-shira, who had saved the new emperor's life when he escaped from the Taychiuts, became a royal aide, along with his sons.

The appointments marked something new in nomadic experience. In the past, unity had always been shattered by tribal rivalries. These had blighted Genghis's own childhood and constantly threatened his slow rise to power. His revolution broke up tribes and clans, and made appointments on the basis not of inherited position within a tribal

---

[2] De Rachewiltz, 'The Title Čingis Qan / Qaɣan Re-Examined'.

GENGHIS'S LEADERSHIP SECRET NO. 7

## MAKE LOYALTY THE PRIME VIRTUE, AND REWARD IT

In a nomadic society, men were free to be their own masters, and free to switch allegiances if they chose. A man might feel bound to an oath of loyalty, or not, depending on how he read his self-interest. For an ambitious leader, loyalty was like gold: hard to find, easily lost. Genghis bound his followers to him by the strength of his integrity. He promised total commitment, and expected it in return. On several occasions, when enemy soldiers came to him having betrayed their leader, he had them executed. When he could, he rewarded his loyal followers – whatever their status – with high office, and booty after a campaign. Once he was khan, well-directed generosity became the bedrock of his administration.

hierarchy but of services rendered. Loyalty was the key. Shepherds, herders and carpenters were included. Two of the most eminent generals were blacksmiths' sons. Jelme, a former servant-boy who had saved Genghis's life by sucking poison from a wound, became commander of a 'thousand'. So did Jebe, a former enemy who had shot Genghis's horse from under him but then devoted himself to his service. They became not *anda*, sworn friends of equal status, for Genghis had seen what happens when equals fall out; they were *nökhörs*, companions, intimates: they shared the khan's life, served him, protected him, advised him, but were always one rung below him. If this was now a feudal society, as many scholars argue, then the *nökhörs* were equivalents to the knights serving an Arthurian Genghis, or the 'companions of the Prophet' in early Islam.

## Tight control from the top down

The system Genghis introduced was ruthlessly centralized, with himself as the fount of all authority. Control depended on two elements, both taken over from other tribes. First, the army was divided into units of tens, hundreds, thousands and ten-thousands, rather as western armies are formed of platoons, companies, regiments and brigades. Second came an idea taken from Toghril – a bodyguard, a sort of Mongolian SS, whose officers would be the sons of commanders, each of whom would bring between three and ten companions, depending on seniority, and one younger brother. This started small, but would in the course of time grow into a force of 'a full ten thousand'. Loyalty may have been the highest virtue, but Genghis was not taking any chances. These sons, plus their younger brothers, would in effect be hostages, ensuring the good behaviour of their fathers.

All of this is laid out in fine – even obsessive – detail in *The Secret History*. Day guards, night guards, quiver-bearers, stewards, elders of companies, responsibilities, seniorities, who does what when: this is not the usual stuff of epic or poetry. To include it is like inserting memos about the administration of Troy into *The Iliad*. For page after page, the only poetry in this tedious account occurs when the *History* wishes to remind us of some character's past adventures with our hero. Yet clearly it was all terribly important, for these are the rules and regulations that define the relationships between the ruler, his staff and his subjects.

There are several points to be made about Genghis's leadership qualities here:

- **He really cared about detail**. This is a remarkable quality in a man apparently focused on achieving power: not simply to have a talent for politics and strategy, but also to be able to focus on the nuts and bolts of management.
- **His decisions made explicit his core values**, principally his high regard for loyalty and his willingness to provide generous rewards for his subordinates.
- **He chose the right people**. These were not men who wanted only to be rich and powerful; they shared his core values and his vision. They included men like Muqali, who would become his viceroy in China, masterminding both conquest and administration in his absence; and Subodei, perhaps one of the greatest generals of all time, who would guide the campaign westward, to the very fringes of Europe. Genghis might have favoured his own sons as generals, but he kept them as nominal leaders only, their task being to inherit his vision of world dominion.
- **All of the above ensured that his people were with him**. There was in them 'the intoxication of the warpath', in John Keegan's phrase. They were warrior-heroes, happy in their mutual admiration, satisfied 'by a shared contempt for a softer world, by the rough comforts of the bivouac, by

competition in endurance'. But this was more than an army: it was a nation forced, then cajoled, then persuaded to adopt a shared vision. Forget for the moment that this vision was brutal, and in the long run completely unrealistic. At the time, and for many years to come, his people were attuned, in leadership-speak. They were like iron filings, aligned by the magnetism of Genghis. Everyone was responsible for fulfilling their part of the bargain with their leader; everyone accepted the need for self-discipline, and rigid discipline, applied down the line. As Goleman puts it: 'When core values and norms are clear to people, a leader does not even need to be physically present for the team to run effectively.'

## Mongols get their first legal system

On this basis, with the new writing system, Genghis could make firm laws. As the Persian historian Juvaini wrote: 'In accordance and in agreement with his own mind he established a rule for every occasion and a regulation for every circumstance; while for every crime he had a fixed penalty.' Shigi became, in effect, justice minister, with responsibility for handing out punishments and recording laws and legal decisions, in 'blue writing', in a book or on scrolls. The laws he recorded would become the framework on which the national and later imperial administration would be based. Shigi's Blue Book became famous as the 'Great Yasa' or *jasakh* (or *zasag*, pronounced 'dzassag', in modern Mongolia: there are various transliterations of the word, which now means ordinance or legal code). On every great occasion, says Juvaini, 'they produce these rolls and model their actions thereon'. Later, the laws, along with 'maxims' or oral comments made by Genghis himself, were turned into verse and recited on great occasions. The rolls themselves vanished – possibly because the code was never printed and never became legal in China even after the Mongol conquest – but elements can be derived from non-Mongol sources.

Several thirteenth- and fourteenth-century historians, Persian, Egyptian and Chinese, confirm that the 'Great Yasa' was indeed a written code, but it was never all-encompassing, and was probably applied quite loosely. Only about 36 laws and 30 maxims survive at second hand, clearly not enough to make up the legal code of an empire. Some are missing entirely, one being the law by which Genghis insisted on controlling all booty; not that he was hungry for wealth himself, but he needed to control the destructive urges of his subordinates, act the generous lord and reward those who deserved it. Those laws we do know about are filtered through other cultures, so they can hardly be said to reflect Genghis's true opinions and character. Some are remarkably liberal. 'All religions were to be respected and no preference was to be shown to any of them'; no prince was to be above the law. Others were designed to enforce order, in draconian fashion: death for theft, adultery, sodomy and sorcery; for failure to pick up and return a bow dropped by the soldier in front of you, failure to return a stolen horse if you happen to find it. Others seem incomprehensibly harsh: death for snooping, urinating into water or ashes, being thrice bankrupt, keeping a runaway slave, killing an animal 'in the Muslim fashion', even stepping on the threshold of a commander's

GENGHIS'S LEADERSHIP SECRET NO. 8

# MAKE FIRM RULES,
# AND MAKE THEM CLEAR

Not much is left today of Genghis's body of laws, but several things are plain: they were intended to replace tribal customary laws; they applied to all Mongols (but not to Chinese or Muslims); and they applied to high and low, irrespective of status – a vital step in establishing Genghis's hold over 'all the people of the felt-walled tents' and aligning them in support of his expansionist policies.

tent. Perhaps these were as fictional as the one quoted by an Armenian authority, which claimed the Yasa told people to love one another, not to commit adultery, not to steal, not to bear false witness, not to be a traitor, and to respect old people and the poor. Was Genghis a closet Christian? Not likely.

Genghis's maxims are an equally odd mixture of good sense and truism, pettiness and imagination. A man who breaks the Yasa time after time must be admonished, then temporarily exiled, then put in irons and imprisoned. A man may get drunk three times a month, and 'if one does not drink at all, what can be better? But where can such a man be found?' Oddly for outsiders, there is nothing about murder being a crime, presumably because, in a feuding society, vengeance was taken by the victim's family, not the state.

One conclusion to be drawn from this arbitrary and distorted collection is that, whatever form the laws took, they were designed to reinforce discipline in the army and the pony express courier service, on which present and future conquests depended. Genghis knew from experience that only the law could guarantee peace and security, but it seems that the mixture of peoples and traditions in his growing empire prevented the code's ruthless application.

## Asserting the supremacy of the state

There was one final step to take to achieve total power. As yet, Genghis claimed only temporal authority. Yet he also claimed divine support, and this sidelined those who claimed to control access to the will of Heaven: the shamans. His position was comparable to that of Henry VIII, who was the supreme power in the realm, except as head of the church, in which capacity he was subject to the authority of the pope. If king and pope worked together, fine. If not, trouble. When trouble came, the immediate cause was Henry's wish to divorce Catherine of Aragon; but at root the dispute was a struggle to see who was master in England: non-English church or English state, pope or king? It was the same with Genghis. If his claim to divine backing received unstinted shamanic support, fine. If not . . .

Not, as it happened; with dramatic consequences. One of his father's closest friends had seven sons, one of whom was famous as a shaman or magician who could (so it was said) walk naked in winter and make ice steam. His name was Kököchu, followed by a title, Teb Tengeri, which may (scholars argue about it) mean something like All-Divine or Wholly Heavenly. According to one source (Rashid al-Din) he may even have devised the title of Genghis.

Anyway, he claimed to have links with Eternal Heaven, which put him at odds with Genghis's own claim. In addition, he had had a run-in with Genghis's younger brother Jochi, known as Khasar (a sort of wild dog), who was famous for his strength. *The Secret History* turns Khasar into a super-hero:

> *His body is three fathoms high,*
> *And he dines on three-year-old cattle . . .*
> *When he swallows a man complete with quiver,*
> *It does not get stuck in his throat,*
> *When he gulps down a whole man*
> *It does not fill his stomach.*

Now Khasar bore a grudge, because Kököchu and his brothers had ganged up on him and beaten him up. When he complained to his brother, Genghis told him not to make a fuss. 'In the past you have done nothing but claim that you could not be vanquished by any living being. How is it that you have now been vanquished?' Khasar left in tears. Kököchu took full advantage, seeking to turn brother against brother. Remember the heavenly signs foretelling that you would be khan? he said to Genghis. Well, there is another, saying that Khasar will rule. 'If you don't strike at Khasar, there is no knowing what will happen!' Genghis kidnapped Khasar, immobilized him by tying his sleeves, humiliated him by removing his hat and belt, and started to interrogate him.

At this moment Hoelun burst in, 'unable to contain her fury', and subjected Genghis to another dramatic dressing-down. She sat cross-legged, took out both her breasts, laid them over her knees, and said, 'Have you seen them? They are breasts that suckled you,' meaning both brothers. 'Temüjin used to drain this one breast of mine . . . As for Khasar, he completely drained both my breasts and brought me comfort.' You, Temüjin, she ranted on, are clever; Khasar is a great archer, able to subdue all those on the run. Yet now suddenly you say you can no longer bear the sight of him? That almost stopped Genghis. 'I was afraid of Mother getting so angry,' he said and backed off. But that left Khasar bitter and Kökochu untouched, gathering forces of his own, including some defectors from Genghis's family. Another of Genghis's brothers, Temüge, went to demand the return of his people, and got a beating for his temerity. Again, it was a woman – his wife, Börte – who told Genghis that enough was enough, this time goading Genghis until he gave Temüge the nod to do whatever he liked. His chance came when Kökochu came to visit with his father and six brothers, in full public view. Temüge challenged Kökochu to a wrestling match, and dragged him outside into the arms of three strong helpers, who broke Kökochu's back. Kökochu's father and brothers would have attacked and killed Genghis, had not his guards protected him. Genghis commented that Kökochu deserved to die for beating Khasar and spreading slander, and – turning to the seven men – 'you and your sons began thinking that you were equal to me, and you have paid for this'. Moreover, this dispute would end right now. 'If one retracts in the evening what one has said in the morning . . . surely one will only be criticized until he is covered in shame. I have earlier pledged my word to you. Enough of this matter!'

What are we to make of all this? A leader with earthly power and claims to Heavenly backing is challenged by a rival with Heavenly power and claims to earthly ones. To take action prematurely would be to split the tribe. Genghis tolerates various insults, even allows himself to be turned against his brother. Action to arrest the brother is condemned by his mother. The rival gains in confidence. More insults follow. Eventually his wife spurs him to action – an assassination from which he is careful to keep his distance, until it is time to claim justification. There are difficult choices here, and he deals with them by dumping the decisions on his womenfolk, and by evasion. It's a dirty business. He emerges, not with his reputation for decisive action much enhanced, but with his power increased. What was the alternative? To allow the challenge to go unchallenged, to enter another civil war, perhaps to lose and see the nation redivided? No: this is now a leader of cunning, able to bend morality to keep power, and win more.

*This is now a leader of cunning, able to bend morality to keep power, and win more.*

## The need for conquest

Genghis's revolution remade his society. It was now devoted to one purpose: conquest.

And conquest was vital. This was a nation of horsemen – civilians who were also soldiers – primed and ready to go, as dependent on explosive growth as the Huns had been 800 years before, equally untrammelled by any hint of morality in their dealings with other cultures. But the

Mongols possessed something that the Huns did not: an ideology. A reformed society and a nation at arms needs a purpose outside itself, as uncounted leaders have discovered down the ages. A leader in these circumstances could hardly tell his people to settle down, go back to their herds and contemplate the infinite. His people had peace. Now they needed more:

- **Security**. National unity had brought them internal security. But Mongol unity was a danger to Jin, whose foreign policy had been dedicated to the business of recruiting 'barbarians to control barbarians'. Now, suddenly, one lot of barbarians had blotted up all the others. Any Jin emperor of spirit would see that this was a threat that could not be allowed to stand. Genghis had to get his retaliation in first.
- **Wealth**. There was no source of wealth locally, no 'peace dividend' in the sheep trade. This was not a money economy. Troops could not be paid, except in kind. Once the conquered tribes had been absorbed – the men allocated to their regiments, the young women distributed, the children taken as slaves, the silks, goblets, saddles, bows, horses and herds all shared out – the warriors looked at their leader with new expectations.

Genghis therefore had the advantage that his troops were now naturally aligned behind him. There are other reasons, too, why ordinary fighting men would do his bidding. These reasons have been well analysed by Norman Dixon in his witty but also deeply serious book *On the Psychology of Military Incompetence*. How is it, he asks, that troops have so often obeyed idiot commanders? How can troops overlook palpable egocentricity, glaring incompetence and utter negligence (displayed, for instance, by several notorious British commanders in the Crimean War and the First World War)? He offers several answers. First, war is a stressful business, and under stress men accept, indeed actually prefer, autocratic leadership they would never accept in civilian life. This is especially true if their leaders take risks and lead from the front. In the peculiar circumstances of war 'there is an understandable urge to clutch at straws – the good aspects of a leader are seized upon, the less good conveniently denied'. Second, military organizations recall an authoritarian family group in which the father-figure has absolute rule: soldiers act like children and do as they are told. If this explains the success of incompetent leaders with little feeling for their suffering troops, how much more is it true of great ones, like Alexander, or Nelson – or Genghis.

Old ways had been broken, new ones forged – to be pursued how, exactly? Only by looking to the ultimate source of wealth, which would also be the source of future challenges: the settled lands to the south, beyond the Gobi.

# 4

# COMMANDER:
# FIRST STEPS IN
# EMPIRE-BUILDING

G ENGHIS HAD already been three types of leader – warlord, politician and social reformer – all of which were rooted in his performance as the warrior-hero. Throughout his life, he prided himself on his nomad toughness and austerity, on his refusal to be made soft by luxury. He could, of course, ride with the best, and fight as they did, with bow-and-arrow and sword. He was already the veteran of countless battles and skirmishes. Risking his life had been second nature for years. He had been wounded at least twice by arrows, but such wounds were as routine as the injuries sustained by a prize-fighter. These were badges of honour, showing he was more than an equal for his bold companions, 'men whose worth in their own eyes and those of their equals was determined by disregard for danger and contempt for the future'. The words are those of the military historian John Keegan, writing of Alexander. He continues: 'The knowledge that their king was taking the supreme risk drove capable and well-briefed subordinates, at the head of drilled and self-confident troops, to fight as hard and skilfully as if he had been at the elbow of each one of them.' Like him, Genghis must have been 'brave with the bravery of the man who disbelieves his own mortality'. This, perhaps, is the result if you feel your mission and leadership are backed by Heaven. It is certainly a necessary attribute if you wish to retain the loyalty of your commanders and troops.

Now he faced something new. Even if he had been content to rule his new nation in peace, it would not have been content with him if he had. He did not even consider the possibility of peaceful coexistence, or of defence. He was like the driver of a chariot who suddenly finds himself in charge of runaways, at the head of a people and an army hungry for action and booty. His task was to provide direction, fast, if he was to fulfil his promises. And he had to ensure victory. This meant becoming a strategist, on an international scale, but a strategist of a rather limited sort. He had no thought of seizing and occupying territory. The Mongols had no experience of foreign administration; nor were they seeking economic control of trade routes; nor did they want to control scarce resources. Genghis was still a robber-baron, if on a gigantic scale.

There being nothing worth seizing in the Siberian forests to the north, and the far western Islamic cultures being very far away indeed, the direction to look was south, beyond the gravel plains and sands of the Gobi, to what is now north China. This is where the novelty comes in, for robbing on this grand scale would require a new skill: the taking of cities.

It's worth a recap of what lay before him.

China was divided into three empires:

- **Jin** in northern and north-eastern China, a state taken over by Jurchens from Manchuria in 1125. The Jin had destroyed the pre-existing Liao empire and subjugated or expelled Liao's Khitan ruling class.

- **Xi Xia** in the west, spanning present-day Xinjiang. This 300-year-old empire was ruled by Tanguts, who were of Tibetan stock and had a mixed culture of herding and citified sophistication.
- **Song** in southern China, the rump of the once-unified China shattered by the Jurchens' Jin Dynasty invasions of the early twelfth century.

Song was too far away to contemplate. Genghis's choice was between Jin and Xi Xia. Jin was the Mongols' old enemy, to which they paid a customary tribute every year. Jin had to be the main target, because that was where the booty lay. Since seizing their empire in 1125, the Jurchen had rapidly adopted Chinese ways, with a love not only of art and theatre but also of silks and textiles and fine clothing and slaves and women: just the sort of luxury despised and desired by Mongols in equal measure. It was Jin that had condemned Genghis's ancestor Ambakai to a grisly death, nailed to a 'wooden donkey'. Vengeance and booty: that, for the present, was inspiration enough. And speed was of the essence, in case Jin saw the dangers of a unified Mongolia, and mounted a pre-emptive strike against the upstart nomads.

Genghis, like any good military (or corporate) strategist, depended crucially on intelligence about his enemies. This he had in abundance. Indeed, one Chinese source, Mengda Beilu, who visited Mongolia when Genghis was building his empire, says that Genghis 'had in his youth been captured by Jin, and served more than 10 years as a slave. Only then did he flee home. Therefore he had an

## GENGHIS'S LEADERSHIP SECRET NO. 9

# GET REAL

Four times in his military career, Genghis faced forces that should have been vastly superior to his own armies: Xi Xia, Jin, Khorazm, Xi Xia 2; after his death his heirs finished off Jin (Jin 2) and took Song. Such operations are always risky; but much less so if intelligence is sound and interpretations unbiased. Numerous military disasters have shown what happens if these are lacking, as Norman Dixon concludes. Examples include the British defeats in the Afghan War of 1841–2, in the Crimea (1857) and in South Africa (1898); and the American catastrophes when Japan attacked Pearl Harbor in 1941 and US forces failed to take Cuba with their assault at the Bay of Pigs in 1961. More recent critics would also cite the US invasion of Iraq. All these show that 'even the combined intellects and specialised knowledge of highly intelligent and dedicated men are no proof against decisions so totally unrealistic as subsequently to tax the credulity of even those who had made them'. The result is a suicidal 'groupthink', in the term coined by the psychologist I. L. Janis. Symptoms include an illusion of invulnerability; collective attempts to ignore information that might shake cherished assumptions; an unquestioned belief in the group's inherent morality; stereotyping the enemy; and an illusion of unanimity. Genghis, the underdog, could not afford such faults.

exact knowledge of the workings of the Jin empire.'[1] No other source mentions this, which makes it seem unlikely.

[1] In Meng-Ta Pei-Lu and Hei-Ta Shih-Lüeh, *Chinesische Gesandtenberichte*. This report, probably a distorted version of his capture by the Taychiuts, was seized upon by the Russian director Sergei Bodrov, who made it central to his film *Mongol* (2008), though for dramatic reasons he had Genghis captured not by Jin but by the Tanguts of Xi Xia.

Possibly, it reflects a story told in north China to explain why Genghis was so well informed. But there was no need for stories. Many of Jin's subject Khitans had defected to him with all the intelligence he needed. From them he knew that Jin had been weakened by war with Song (1206–8), an attempted coup, a famine, and opposition from the Jurchen and Chinese masses who were bitterly opposed to foreign rule. A border tribe stood ready to allow the Mongols through the Jin's earthwork versions of the Great Wall. A surly populace, a weakened army, porous defences, disenchanted officers: why, Jin would tumble with one good push.

Feeling himself justified by ancient enmity, Genghis sought confrontation. In 1208 an heir to the Jin throne, Prince Weishao, came to the border to meet Genghis, expecting to receive the usual tribute with much attendant ritual. He was greeted with much-reduced ritual, and no tribute. This insult should really have been cause enough for war, but the Jin emperor had enough on his plate. The following year he died, and Prince Wei succeeded. When an ambassador brought the news, Genghis was expected to kowtow. Instead he said, 'I thought the ruler of the Middle Kingdom came from Heaven. Can he be a person of such weakness as Prince Wei? Why should I kowtow to him?' Saying which, he 'faced south, spat, mounted his horse and rode off towards the north'. He might as well have declared war there and then.

But a direct assault would have been foolish. Jin had a population of 40 million and an army of 600,000, almost ten times Genghis's. Besides, Jin might call upon Xi Xia for help against a force that could be presented as a threat to all in the region. Best to deal with the lesser, then – with his power increased by Heaven and Earth, as he put it – go for the greater. There would have been no thought of occupation, only a vague plan, probably, to use Xi Xia's wealth as a stepping stone to seizing or extorting yet more wealth from Jin, and forestalling any possibility of an assault.

# The hunt as war-game

Now ruler of all the Mongol tribes, Genghis commanded a formidable army, well trained in manoeuvres and rapid communication by the practice of hunting on a massive scale, a form of training common to all pastoral nomads over the previous thousand years. Indeed, so vital was this activity that it calls into question the term 'pastoral nomadism'; Genghis's people were really pastoral nomadic hunters. Each clan, each tribe, each new federation undertook these hunts, which covered ever greater areas with every increase in the size of the political unit. The hunt started in autumn, when game was fat from the late summer glut. Scouts – acting as spies in this war-game – would report on the wealth of game. Then horsemen gathered by the thousand and spread out in an immense line extending over perhaps 100 kilometres – left wing, centre, right wing, as if in battle formation, with arrows and food supplies to last them many days, perhaps weeks. The line gradually formed itself into a circle, with one mounted archer every few metres. Juvaini, the great Persian historian who worked for the Mongol empire some 30 years after Genghis's death, gives a powerful account of the great *av*, or hunt (called a battue in western languages, from the French for 'beaten') and its significance for military organization and discipline:

For a month, or two, or three they form a hunting ring and drive the game slowly and gradually before them, taking care lest any escape from the ring. And if, unexpectedly, any game should break through, a minute inquiry is made into the cause and reason, and the commanders of thousands, hundreds and tens are clubbed therefor, and often even put to death ... For two or three months, by day and by night, they drive the game in this manner, like a flock of sheep, and dispatch messages to the khan to inform him of the condition of the quarry, its scarcity or plenty, whither it has come and from whence it has been started. Finally when the ring has been contracted to two or three parasangs [about 10–15 kilometres], they bind ropes together and cast felts over them; while the troops come to a halt all around the ring, standing shoulder to shoulder. The ring is now filled with the cries and commotion of every manner of game and the roaring and tumult of every kind of ferocious beast.

Then the killing starts, initiated by the khan and his retinue, followed by the princes, officers and finally the troops, until only 'wounded and emaciated stragglers' are left. At this point, old men humbly beg the khan for the lives of the survivors, so that their numbers can recover from the cull. The hunt ends with a head-count and distribution of the spoils for food and furs.

'Now war,' says Juvaini, 'with its killing, counting of the slain and sparing of the survivors, is after the same fashion, and indeed analogous in every detail.' Edward Gibbon in his *Decline and Fall of the Roman*

GENGHIS'S LEADERSHIP SECRET NO. 10

# IN PEACE,
# TRAIN FOR WAR

Nomadic clans had always practised large-scale hunts –
battues – as preparation for war, circling wild animals as if
they were foot soldiers. This training gave the Mongols an
advantage unavailable to urban societies, in which large-
scale training for war would have been both expensive and
unrealistic. Chinese writers on war focused mainly on
leadership, strategy and discipline, with little to say about
training. For urban societies, the only true training was
war itself. In nomadic societies, the battue served many
purposes: it was a pleasure, an exercise in cooperation, an
extension of an everyday activity, and self-financing in
that it provided every participant with game. It also
involved slaughter on a grand scale, which is not training
usually available until the heat of battle.

*Empire* makes the same point, in his usual sonorous style:

> In this march, which frequently continues many
> days, the cavalry are obliged to climb the hills, to
> swim the rivers, and wind through the valleys with-
> out interrupting the prescribed order of their
> gradual progress. They acquired the habit of direct-
> ing the eye and their steps to remote objects, of
> preserving their intervals, of suspending or acceler-
> ating their pace to the motions of their troops on
> their right and left, and of watching and repeating
> the signals of their leaders . . . To employ against a

human enemy the same patience and valour, the
same skill and discipline, is the only alteration
which is required in real war, and the amusements
of the chase serve as a prelude to the conquest of an
empire.

No wonder, then, that by the time of the invasion of Xi
Xia, no other army in history had ever (in Juvaini's words)
been 'so patient of hardship, so grateful for comforts, so
obedient to its commanders both in prosperity and
adversity; and this not in hope of wages and fiefs nor in
expectation of income or promotion. This, indeed, is the
best way to organize an army.'

No hunt and no war had been conducted by the
Mongols on this scale. What army in the whole world can
equal the Mongol army? asks Juvaini. In action, the warriors are like trained wild beasts, in peace like sheep, in
misfortune free of dissension. They contribute without
complaint. They can all become herdsmen, swordsmen,
archers and lancers as occasion demands. They display
their equipment on demand, and accept punishment if
they fall short. Each man toils as much as the next, with
no attention being paid to wealth and power. No one leaves
his unit and joins another without permission. The hunt
honed their qualities, giving them practice in long-range
communication, coordinating movement over differing
landscapes, applying complex rules about the distribution
of the booty and – perhaps most crucially – striking a
difficult balance between obeying orders and taking the
initiative to cope with local conditions. And all this,
remember, had to be arranged with men of different
kinship groups, different tribes, different languages. No

wonder that when three Mongol leaders pledged themselves to Genghis, they promised:

*For you we shall drive the beasts of the steppe*
*Until their bellies press together.*

Such conformity sounds like a form of indoctrination; but
to those involved, recalling the recent past of feuding
and deprivation, it must have seemed an escape into a
world of inclusion, power, status, success and
undreamed-of wealth. In any event, the capacity to
mobilize such an army was proof of Genghis's astonishing
ability to inspire and control his people.

## Taking out the weakest link

In spring 1209 came the invasion of Xi Xia, across the Gobi
for 500 kilometres to the Three Beauties mountains. Here
the Altai mountains finally end in three ranges of peaks,
canyons, high pastures, sand and gravel. The Three
Beauties, now a national park, would have made a good
staging post. From here, the route led on southward
another 300 kilometres to the Helan mountains, which
run south between the Yellow River and the Alashan
desert. When the Mongols seized a little fortress town, the
Tanguts asked for help from Jin, who were expected to
come to the Tanguts' aid against a common enemy. But Jin

was in new hands, those of the inexperienced Prince Wei – the same prince despised by Genghis for his lack of spirit and judgement – who told the Tangut ruler: 'It is to our advantage when our enemies attack one another. Wherein lies the danger to us?'

Driving on south, desert to their right, mountains to their left, the Mongols came to a fortress defending the only pass leading through the Helan mountains to the Tangut capital, present-day Yinchuan. After a two-month stand-off, the Mongols lured the Tanguts into battle, and won a stunning victory. The way to Yinchuan was open.

Now they faced a problem. Yinchuan was well defended, and the Mongols had never tried to take a city before. They had no triple-bow siege engines, as the Song and Jin did, no catapults, no incendiary bombs, no captured experts to teach them about siege warfare. A strategy suggested itself: they would break Yinchuan's ancient canal system, which led water from the Yellow River to irrigate the city's fertile plains. Not a good idea. The terrain here is as flat as Holland. Flood waters did little damage to the city, but spread over Yinchuan's flat agricultural land and forced the Mongols back to higher ground.

To break the impasse, both gave ground. The Tangut emperor submitted, giving a daughter in marriage to Genghis, and handing over camels, falcons and textiles as tribute. Genghis, certain that he now had a compliant vassal, ordered a withdrawal.

Perhaps that was the best he could have done. But, as events would show, it was not good enough. The Tanguts, with every reason to hate the Mongols, were still very much alive, to resume the fight another day. This was a smash-and-grab raid, but it ended – to switch analogies – not in a knock-out but in a win on points. Genghis departed thinking he had a compliant new vassal. He was wrong; but he would not discover that for another eight years.

## Terror – and beyond

With his right wing secure, Genghis could plan the assault on Jin. As it turned out, it would be not one assault, but three, because the Mongols were not ready to assault in the right way. Their leader, dynamic though he was, had not yet responded to – perhaps not even seen – the real challenge of building an empire.

In the spring of 1211 the Mongols, crossing the Gobi as if it were a bridge not a barrier, shattered the Jin cavalry guarding the pass leading down from the highlands, then stormed the final pass that guards the approach to Beijing. Other columns headed south to the Yellow River and east into Manchuria. For Genghis, this was victory enough. He withdrew, not yet willing to contemplate the next stage of conquest: total victory, the seizure of cities, the occupation of territory, the administration of empire.

More attacks came the following year – called off when Genghis sustained another arrow-wound – and again in 1213, this time driving a sword into the heart of the Jin empire in an attempt to force it to capitulate and become a vassal. The key town of Datong fell. Two commanders fled their posts. 'The army's morale is the essential element in warfare,' commented the Jin history. 'The spirit of resolution was lost and could not be regained. The collapse of the Jin was foretold in this event.'[2] Mongols, pillaging at will over the north China plain, seized food from a starving population. While a small force pinned down Beijing's 36,000 defenders, three Mongol armies swept through the outlying regions, each one supported and protected by the other two in a giant chess game at which the Jin were hopelessly outclassed. This time cities tumbled, often because the Mongols drove captives ahead of them pushing siege engines to the walls, thus forcing a dreadful choice on the inhabitants: kill their own, or surrender.

Still Beijing held out, for it had formidable defences. Outside the walls were four self-sufficient fortress-villages linked to the capital by tunnels. Three moats protected the walls, which formed a rectangle some 15 kilometres around. A crenellated parapet rose 12 metres above the ground, with 13 gates and a guard tower every 15 metres: over 900 of them in all. The inhabitants deployed immense crossbows, catapults that could lob 25-kilo boulders, fire-arrows, fire-balls of burning wax, explosive ceramic shells, pots of flaming naphtha, flame-throwers using petroleum, even chemical bombs filled with chemicals and excrement. If the Mongols were to take and hold cities, these weapons would have to be seized and mastered.

Despite several assaults, Genghis's troops failed to take the city. Clearly, it would starve if the siege continued. But the Mongols, too, were suffering from camping out, in winter, in a ravaged countryside. Early in 1214 Genghis offered to withdraw – if the terms were right. Wei having been deposed, the new emperor agreed to hand over a princess, 500 boys and girls, 3,000 horses and 10,000 rolls of silk. As *The Secret History* puts it: 'As for the satin and

[2] Mote, *Imperial China*, p. 244.

goods, our troops loaded as much as their horses could carry and moved away, tying up their loads with bands of heavy silk fabric.'

Genghis ordered his booty-laden troops back north to the welcoming grasslands, thinking, once again, that he had won a compliant vassal. Jin was a wreck, its prestige destroyed, and Genghis, with victories over the two great powers of northern China, was the region's greatest leader. Was this not total success?

No, it wasn't. He had made the same error in both Xi Xia and Jin. The emperors were left alive and free, the capitals untaken. Moreover, as soon as he departed the Jin reoccupied the very towns and passes that the Mongols had seized, sometimes more than once. Tactically, the campaign had been a brilliant success. Strategically, it was lunacy, and Genghis soon learned the consequences.

That July, the Jin emperor took full advantage of Genghis's retreat. He abandoned Beijing, moving himself and his government 600 kilometres south to the ancient Chinese capital of Kaifeng. This was an epic undertaking: 3,000 camels laden with treasure and 30,000 cartloads of documents and royal possessions, trailing southward for two months. There would be no chance of Genghis demanding anything more of the emperor, unless he took the whole country.

Genghis was aghast at the news. A Chinese source records his words: 'The Jin Emperor . . . has used the peace to deceive me!' It would also have struck him that he had been granted a terrific opportunity: Beijing abandoned by its government, and the countryside full of mutinous troops ready to fight for the Mongols. But he had to act fast, before Kaifeng could become a base for a new Jin offensive. A month later, the Mongols were back at the walls of Beijing.

Pause for a moment to see what power Genghis now held in his hands. Up to this point, the flood of war had mostly flowed from the poor lands of the north to the rich lands of the south. But, like a storm-surge, the waves had ebbed again, barred by city walls and limited by the poverty of the invaders. Now, with the Mongols united, the flood was here to stay. Military victories and large-scale invasion applied new leverage, an ability to accumulate food, goods and captives from the countryside, which made deeper penetration possible, a possibility that so far Genghis had failed to exploit. It opened the way to the capture of cities, cut off from their roots by devastating the surrounding countryside. This deliberate use of pillage and terror would force inhabitants to surrender, to avoid the short-term destruction of their relatives and livelihoods and the long-term fate of starvation. And surrender would supercharge the business of conquest by supplying the tools of large-scale siege warfare: the weapons, the know-how and the people. Under Genghis's leadership,

*Under Genghis's leadership, Mongolia had become a machine for the unprecedented and systematic seizure of wealth.*

Mongolia had become a machine for the unprecedented and systematic seizure of wealth, but with a deeper strategic purpose still to be defined.

There was no attempt to assault Beijing. As the autumn of 1214 turned to winter, the Mongol army just sat tight through the bitter cold. Two relief columns from Kaifeng were smashed and seized by the Mongols. Beijing began to starve. The living ate the dead. The city's civilian commander committed suicide; the military commander fled to Kaifeng (where he was executed for treachery). It still took almost a year to break the deadlock. Only at the end of May 1215 did the leaderless and starving citizens open the gates in surrender.

Genghis, meanwhile, had decamped to the grasslands, some 320 kilometres away by the usual roundabout route through north China's chaotic mountains, to a place close to where his grandson, Kublai, would build his summer palace, Xanadu (Shang-du). Without his restraining influence, the Mongols ran wild. They ransacked the city and killed thousands. The palace went up in flames, and part of the city burned for a month.

## Controlling the spoils of war

At this point, Genghis was confronted with a major problem concerning conquest. Formerly, if a tribal chief made a conquest, everyone got an immediate share of the booty, though technically tradition dictated that the boss owned it all, and gave the nod to its distribution. With the nation's foundation, Genghis had asserted his right to own and allocate the booty, which he needed in order to distribute rewards and act the generous lord. Now, suddenly, a whole capital city had fallen, and he was not even there to supervise. So he had an intense interest in exactly what had come into his possession. He ordered three

GENGHIS'S LEADERSHIP SECRET NO. 11

## MAKE YOUR INTERESTS
## THE STATE'S INTERESTS

Genghis presented himself as the simple nomad, despising luxury. But he also claimed the right to dispense all booty. He could thus set an example of austerity, while also being a fount of wealth for his followers. This is the key to Genghis's leadership, part of what *The Secret History* calls the 'great norm': obedience and loyalty from below, protection and rewards from above. The leader was both an individual and more than an individual – he was the symbol of the state and its laws. Disloyalty to Genghis was treason, and so was the withholding of booty, which denied the right of the leader to dispense rewards, and was therefore a betrayal of both the leader and the state.

senior officers to make an inventory, one of the three being the Tatar Shigi, a natural choice, since he was an adopted member of Genghis's family and also expert in writing, records and administration.

The city's viceroy, Hada, tried to ingratiate himself with them by offering 'gold-embroidered and patterned satins'. Now Genghis's skill in nurturing talent and loyalty paid off. Shigi's two colleagues were all for taking what Hada offered. Wait, said Shigi. Like everything else in the city, the satins had belonged to the Jin emperor, and now the city and all its contents belonged to the conqueror, Genghis. This stuff was not Hada's to give. 'How can you give us the goods and satins of Genghis Khan,' he asked, 'stealing them and bringing them here behind his back?'

With the inventory made, the three reported to

Genghis, and Shigi made his point about ownership. Genghis 'mightily rebuked' the other two, and was delighted with Shigi's judgement. He had been 'mindful of the great norm concerning one's obligations to the khan'. A vital legal precedent had been established. If Genghis was a robber-baron still, he was also much more: a leader who had chosen to operate according to recorded laws, imposing strict discipline, applied by people who all understood what he was about. These were yet further steps towards true empire.

The campaign also marked another step forward: the taking of a major city. This had always been a problem for nomadic peoples, indeed for any force that lacked the technology of large-scale assault. Now Genghis had the solution: terror and scorched earth. The secret was to isolate towns by dominating the countryside, cutting the city from its support system. It was like poisoning the roots of flowering plants. This was similar to the technique Mao adopted when fighting to take over China with an army of the poor before 1949: to draw out the war, use 'the masses', avoid fighting unless victory was certain, and blockade cities into surrender. There were many differences, of course, one being that Mao used terror against the very people he was leading. But the fundamental idea worked, for both leaders. A secondary advantage for Genghis was that ravaging a countryside not only deprived the enemy of sustenance; it provided the means to go on conquering, as region after region gave up its wealth, and city after city opened its gates.

Now the Mongols were masters of all north-east China, cutting the Jin empire by a third, and in half, leaving two rumps: south of the Yellow River and Manchuria. In the newly conquered territories, the few towns still holding out surrendered. Surviving garrisons revolted against their former masters, and declared for the new ones. A million fled south, through devastation and famine, into the Jin heartland south of the Yellow River, where a discredited dynasty collapsed into chaos. With the wealth, military expertise and manpower that he now controlled, Genghis would surely have intended to complete the conquest.

In the event, this would be undertaken by Genghis's heirs, because his attention was seized by events far to the west, which demanded leadership of a totally different order.

# 5

# STRATEGIST: EXPANSION WESTWARD

W E NOW come to one of the most extraordinary campaigns in history, the Mongol conquest of much of the Islamic world. It is perhaps the most extreme example of brilliance and brutality combined. After the slow and often repeated conquests in China, Genghis now emerged as a genius of military strategy, all the more remarkable in that he had not, as far as we know, planned this assault before it was forced upon him.

To understand what happened, we have to look 2,500 kilometres to the west, beyond the deserts of Xinjiang and over the Tien Shan, to a state founded by Khitans after they were chased by the Jurchen from their base in north China in the early twelfth century. Kara Khitai, Black 'Cathay', was centred on present-day Kyrgyzstan, but larger. In the chaos sparked by Genghis's rise to power, refugees streamed into Kara Khitai. One was Kuchlug, prince of the Naimans, a tribe defeated by Genghis. He seized power and turned brutally tyrannical, alienating his new Muslim subjects. Clearly, in Genghis's eyes, he was an unstable fanatic who would be a threat again one day. He had to be eliminated.

In 1217, with part of north China secured, Genghis turned his attention to Kuchlug, entrusting the campaign to Jebe. His advance was more like a migration than an assault: 20,000 men with up to five remounts each – that's 100,000 horses – covering 50 kilometres a day for two months, across grasslands and mountains to Kuchlug's capital. It sounds a high-risk operation, but in fact it wasn't. From his Uighur employees and allies, whose homeland in western China abutted Kara Khitai, Genghis was sure that the Mongols would be welcomed as liberators. So it turned out. At the Mongols' approach, Kuchlug fled 400 kilometres south to the Silk Road emporium of Kashgar, then on to the foothills of the Pamirs, where some local bounty-hunters caught him and handed him over for execution. Thus, in 1218, did Genghis acquire another wing to his growing empire.

Victory put Genghis into contact with Kuchlug's Islamic neighbour, Khorazm,[1] a kingdom straddling much of present-day Uzbekistan and Turkmenistan, and spreading into Iran and Afghanistan. This unruly region had been taken from its nominal overlord, the caliph in Baghdad, half a century before. It controlled several of the great Silk Road cities, among them Samarkand and Bukhara. Khorazm's ruler, Mohammed, had concluded a brief alliance with Kuchlug, and must have watched the Mongol assault on his ally with growing anxiety.

The keys to what follows were two characters: Genghis's, of course, and that of Khorazm's shah, Mohammed. In many ways Mohammed was Genghis's opposite, a catastrophically bad leader with numerous character faults: dominated by his mother, brutal, and a notorious libertine. Politically, he was insecure, a Turk at

---

[1] Also spelled Khwarazm, Khwarizm, Khwarezm and Khorezm.

odds with his mainly Iranian people as well as with the caliph.

Genghis had no interest in embroiling himself in this mess. After all, north China had not yet been fully conquered. There was no need for further conflict in the west, at least not yet. 'In those days,' says the thirteenth-century Persian historian Juvaini, 'the Mongols regarded the Muslims with the eye of respect, and for their dignity and comfort would erect them clean tents of white felt.' All seemed set fair. Three merchants from Bukhara had arrived in Mongolia eager to exploit the route that had suddenly opened up with the Mongol advances into north China. When they returned, Genghis had them accompanied by a huge trade delegation of 100 (as *The Secret History* records),[2] all Muslims except for a Mongol ambassador as leader, to set up business in Islamic lands.

In the winter of 1218–19 the delegation arrived in Otrar, on the Syr Darya river (today's Otyrar, in western Kazakhstan). The merchants carried a message to the sultan from Genghis, stating that they came 'in order that they may acquire the wondrous wares of those regions; and that henceforth the abscess of evil thoughts may be lanced by the improvement of relations'. Or something like that. There are various versions of this message, none suggesting overt hostility. Yet Mohammed took offence, probably assuming that the traders were also spies (possibly true, because Genghis was always hungry for information), and that spies were a necessary prelude to war (not true). Otrar's governor, the other villain in this story, is referred to as Inalchuk, Little Lord. He was a relative of Mohammed's

---

[2] Muslim sources say 450, but 100 is more widely accepted.

dominating mother. Pride and arrogance were his undoing. With a nod and a wink from his overlord, he accused the merchants of spying, and arrested them all.

Though appalled at this insult, Genghis refused to be provoked, for he was a man who knew how to balance anger and restraint. He sent three envoys, who gave Mohammed a chance to disclaim all knowledge of his governor's act and hand him over for punishment. Mohammed foolishly chose to add insult to insult. He had at least one of the envoys, and possibly all three, killed. And then came a third outrage, against the 100 arrested merchants: 'Without pausing to think,' writes Juvaini, 'the Sultan sanctioned the shedding of their blood and deemed the seizure of their goods to be lawful.' 'Little Lord' Inalchuk killed the whole delegation – and these, remember, were all Muslims, except for the leader. Juvaini laments the rashness of an act that, as events showed, 'desolated and laid waste a whole world'.

To kill a single merchant on an official mission, let alone 100 of them, would have been ground enough for war. Even worse was the murder of an ambassador. One of the men contrived to escape 'by a stratagem', and brought the news to Genghis. Juvaini describes him flying into a whirlwind of rage, the fire of wrath driving the water from his eyes so that it was only to be quenched by the shedding of blood. Even so, it took him a while to decide on his course of action: notice the way he subjects his anger to the need to make a considered decision. He 'went alone to the summit of a hill, bared his head, turned his face towards the earth and for three days and nights offered up prayer, saying: "I was not the author of this trouble; grant me strength to exact vengeance."'

These events marked yet another new phase in Genghis's career. There had been many novelties already; all, however, had been part of his agenda. This was entirely unforeseen. No nomad chief would ever willingly have undertaken the task of subduing an empire so far from home, with a vastly greater army than his own. But he had as little choice as an eighteenth-century aristocrat challenged to a duel. He had been personally humiliated. The very basis of his authority was under attack. If – as he was beginning to believe – the Mongols' Heaven-sent destiny was world rule, then this was an outright denial of divine will. If the insult was not avenged, he was finished. The Mongols would become targets for an ambitious sultan eager to exploit their weakness for expansion, and he would find himself on the defensive. As *The Secret History* says, he had no doubts about what had to be done: 'How can my "golden halter" [by which he meant his claim to authority over all peoples on earth] be broken by the Sartagul [Muslim] people?' And he said,

I shall set out against the Sartagul people

*To take revenge,*
*To requite the wrong*
*For the slaying of my hundred envoys.*

## Naming a successor

According to *The Secret History*, this new turning point – an immense investment, a huge risk for his people and himself – inspired a debate on the subject of succession. For any leader, this is a tricky area. Many do not like to consider an end to their rule. Perhaps Genghis, too, avoided the issue, for scholars believe this section is a later addition, interpolated to assert the validity of his successor's claim. But even if he came to the decision later, these events surely reflect his concern.

The problem was posed by the Tatar Yisui, his most senior wife after Börte, who was now in her late fifties and beginning to take a back seat as an adviser. Yisui had been taken after the defeat of her tribe, and was now a fully integrated Mongol. 'Living things who are but born to this world are not eternal,' she said,

> When your body, like a great old tree,
> Will fall down,
> To whom will you bequeath your people?

Genghis saw the point. Once again, a woman had pointed him in the right direction, and he was secure enough to give her acknowledgement. 'Even though she is only a woman, Yisui's words are more right than right . . . no one has advised me like this.' It was as if he had been asleep, he said, 'as if I would not be caught by death'.

How to solve the problem? By custom, his heir would be the clan's senior member – if he could assert the claim. Perhaps, though, seniority would not produce the best candidate. Best not to risk either an inadequate ruler or civil strife. An empire was at stake, not simply a clan. Who better to succeed him than one of his sons, all experienced commanders in their own right? But which one? Customary practice was not much help. An eldest son sometimes laid claim to a father's authority, but the youngest inherited his 'hearth', that is, his tents, his servants, his herds.

Genghis did not simply impose a solution, which would merely have alienated the losers and stored up trouble for later. He opened the problem to all four, in public. This sparked a terrible row. First, what of Jochi, the eldest? But Jochi could have been fathered by a Merkit when his mother was a captive. Chagadai, the second son, burst out: 'How can we let ourselves be ruled by this bastard?' Jochi seized his brother by the collar: 'I have never been told by my father the khan that I was different from my brothers. How can you discriminate against me? In what skill are you better? Only in your obstinacy.' A shaman made peace, reminding them of the dire times into which they had been born: the chaos of a disunited people, their mother's abduction, the fact that they came from the same womb, the way she had suffered for them, the joint work for unity. At this Chagadai smiled, and the two made it up, agreeing that the third son, Ogedei, was steady and reliable. Tolui, the fourth son, nodded: he would be Ogedei's adviser. So it was decided.

Now, all of this is a remarkable tribute to Genghis as leader. Great innovators often have a problem letting go. History, politics and business offer countless examples of leaders who, jealous of their power, select compliant subordinates, refuse to contemplate an ordered succession, and remain obsessed with their own status until the end. It's a problem with big egos: leaders who care more about themselves than their group, their company, their party, their nation, their people.

This was the best Genghis could do. Ogedei would eventually prove too fond of drink, and die of it. But for the moment, the clan and the nation remained united, with firm political foundations for expansion westward.

GENGHIS'S LEADERSHIP SECRETS NOS 12 AND 13

## CHOOSE AN HEIR;
## ALLOW DEBATE

Genghis allowed a respected wife to arm-twist him into nominating an heir. It would, of course, have to be a son. Though several women were to become politically powerful, in 1219 this was still a male-dominated society that needed to balance political rule with military generalship. There was no easy solution, and an intense debate took place before the third son Ogedei emerged as a compromise candidate. It was not ideal; but, by allowing dissent, Genghis took the family with him, and kept the lords of his new nation behind him.

# Hiring the best talent

Genghis, commanding a campaign that needed meticulous planning, wanted help, and as a result was guided to a higher level of leadership.

He already had his companions, his *nökhörs*, to help with the military aspects of the campaign. What no Mongol leader had ever tackled before was the administration of conquered territory. Genghis must already have seen how foolish it was to undertake the same conquest time after time, as he had in China. Conquest should surely be secured with long-term rule. Shigi and perhaps a few of the younger Mongol princes had a rudimentary idea of administration, having learned the Uighur script adopted in 1204. But there was as yet no bureaucracy.

Now Genghis, or perhaps Shigi, recalled one of the

prisoners taken in Beijing three years before, when Shigi had made an inventory of the imperial treasure and notable captives. Among the Jin officials one had stood out, literally: a very tall young man (supposedly about 6 feet 8 inches), aged 25, with a beard reaching to his waist and a magnificent, sonorous voice. He was a Khitan, one of the people who, as the Liao, had once ruled in north-east China and had been displaced by the Jin. His name was Chucai, and his family, Yelü, was one of the most eminent in the Liao empire. Yelü Chucai was a brilliant student, poet and administrator, who had served his Jin masters throughout the siege of Beijing. In an attempt to make sense of this terrible experience, he went on a Buddhist retreat for three years. Now, older, wiser and calmer, he found himself summoned to Genghis as a possible top administrator.

In an exchange that became famous later, Genghis, expecting gratitude, said to Chucai: 'The Liao and the Jin have been enemies for generations. I have avenged you.'

But instead of agreeing, Chucai replied: 'My father and grandfather both served the Jin respectfully. How can I, as a subject and a son, be so insincere at heart as to regard my sovereign and my father as enemies?'

That was true loyalty, not to an individual but to a system. Genghis was impressed by this direct, self-possessed and clever young man, and offered him the job. 'Long Beard', as Genghis called him, was equally impressed. He saw Genghis's successes as proof that Heaven's Mandate had settled upon him. From now on, Chucai would play an important role in moulding the character of the khan and his empire, to the advantage of all. Choosing the right man, Mongol or non-Mongol, was one of Genghis's supreme talents, and Chucai the Khitan

GENGHIS'S LEADERSHIP SECRET NO. 14

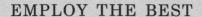

## EMPLOY THE BEST

This is one of those open secrets shared by many top leaders down the ages, and in governments and corporations today. Not all, though. So many leaders don't like the best because they are seen not as an asset but a threat. In the Khitan scholar Yelü Chucai, Genghis found someone with the skills he lacked, but needed. In many ways, Yelü was better than Genghis: literate, widely read, experienced in administration and the ways of Chinese government. He was the best among many non-Mongols, for Genghis, who shared few attitudes with successful modern executives, had this in common with them: he was all for diversity if it helped the cause. And Chucai had another great quality: not only did he have the right skills, he also had the right attitude. Genghis's success convinced him that the Mongol khan was preordained by Heaven for conquest and imperial rule. In his book *On Leadership*, Allan Leighton quotes Earl Sasser of Harvard Business School: 'Attitudes can seldom be taught, whereas skills can.' Chucai would teach both, to Mongols and non-Mongols alike.

was one of his best choices, with life-saving consequences.

Sixteen years later, seven years after Genghis's death, when the rest of north China finally fell to Genghis's heir, Ogedei, the elite discussed what to do with their new acquisition and its 10 million peasant farmers. Some dyed-in-the-wool traditionalists saw no problem: kill the lot, and turn their farms to pasture. It was Chucai who pointed out that taxation and good husbandry would yield far more wealth than yet more death and destruction. He won, and millions lived who might otherwise have died.

By a happy coincidence, or brilliant choice, or Heaven's will, Yelü Chucai came into Genghis's life just in time to offer guidance on the crisis in the west; armed with his advice, Genghis became for the first time a master strategist, with devastating consequences. As a result of his studies, Chucai would have been able to present the essence of Sun Zi's *Art of War*, which sprang from the fourth-century BC heart of the turbulent Warring States period.[3] Rejecting the displays of heroism and vengeance in which warlords like the younger Genghis had indulged, Sun Zi advises total, ice-cool, dedicated, focused professionalism. Set passion aside: 'A sovereign must not launch a war because he is enraged, nor can a general fight a war because he is resentful. For while an angered man may again be happy, and a resentful man again be pleased, a state that has perished cannot be restored, nor can the dead be brought back to life.'

Cool professionalism involves more than practical consideration of the 'five fundamentals' – politics, weather, terrain, command and management. The wise commander remembers that, whatever the motive for war, the aim is not to indulge in destruction but to win, fast, with as little risk and damage to oneself as possible. 'While we have heard of stupid haste in war, we have not seen a clever operation that was prolonged ... What is valued in war is victory, not prolonged operations.'

Forget also indulgence in cruelty, and love of violence, for to benefit from victory you must make use of your enemy. 'In war, the best policy is to take a state intact; to

---

[3] Sun Zi is rendered Sun Tzu in the older Wade–Giles transliteration system.

ruin it is inferior to this.' Imagine Chucai in the role of a consultant arguing for ideas refined by centuries of experience, many of which must have been totally counter-intuitive to Genghis. In presenting his urgent advice Chucai did not need to summarize Sun Zi, for Sun Zi himself wrote in summary – I am tempted to say PowerPoint – form. All Chucai needed to do was quote him. Listen to him on 'the art of offensive strategy':

> 'Those skilled in war subdue the enemy's army without battle.'
> 'They capture the enemy's cities without assaulting them.'
> 'Their aim is to take all under heaven intact by strategic considerations.'
> 'Thus their troops are not worn out and their gains will be complete.'

This programme would have appalled Genghis's feuding forebears: no grand gestures, no foolhardy displays of bravery, rapine, destruction. But it was an ideal agenda for the conquest of Khorazm – in principle, even if it was modified dramatically in practice by Genghis's brutal but effective strategy for the taking of cities.

The art of war may have been the most pressing of his subjects, but it was only part of Chucai's agenda. He also set Genghis on a very different sort of journey, which must be the subject of a separate chapter.

For the campaign westward, Genghis asked for troops from his vassals in the borderlands of Mongolia, in Uighur lands, in north China, in Manchuria and in

Xi Xia, whose king had promised help when necessary.

What Genghis received in return, however, was a slap in the face as sharp as the one from Khorazm's sultan Mohammed. The slap came not directly from Xi Xia's ruler, but from his military commander or *gambu*, the power behind the throne, Asha. 'If Genghis is really that weak,' he wrote, 'why did he ever bother to become khan?'

But Genghis could not respond to this insult right then. His first task was to march against Mohammed. Once victory had been secured there, then, 'if I am protected by Eternal Heaven,' he would take his revenge on Xi Xia.

## The campaign westward

The army Genghis sent to Khorazm was a different sort of army from the one that had swept across the Gobi into Xi Xia and north China; different also from the one led by Jebe in pursuit of Kuchlug. With some 100,000–150,000 soldiers, each with three or four horses, it kept the fast-moving cavalry units, which could cover 100 kilometres a day, cross deserts, swim rivers, and materialize and vanish as if by magic. But there were also entirely new elements acquired after the sieges of Beijing and other Chinese cities: battering rams, scaling ladders, four-wheeled mobile shields, trebuchets with their many different types of fire- and smoke-bombs, flame-throwing tubes, huge double- and triple-bowed siege engines, perhaps even explosive devices like the 'heaven-shaking thunder', an iron casing filled with gunpowder that blew to bits anyone within 10 or 15 metres.

Such an operation suggests comparison with other large-scale advances, like Alexander's into Asia,

Branch : Gordon
Date : 19/06/2011    Time: 14:21
Name : Girouard, Frederick
ID : T4606460

ITEM(S) BORROWED                DUE DATE

Twenty thousand leagues un...20/07/11
N59329102
Renewals (2)

The black cauldron / [No. ...20/07/11
N5848/715

The book of three : [No. 1 ...20/07/11
N5963885C

The castle of Llyr : [No....20/07/11
N59323807

Please retain this receipt and return
      items before the due date.

Thankyou for using Gordon Library
Phone: 94240909

* * * * * *

Return your items on time to avoid paying a fine

* * * * * *

Author Encounter - Christopher Bevan
6.30 pm Wednesday 6 July 2011
Gordon Library Meeting Room
Bookings essential
Call 9424 0909.

* * * * * * *

Ku-ring-gai Council 9424 0000

Napoleon's to Moscow in 1812, those of the British and German armies duelling across North Africa in the Second World War. The problem with operations like these is one of logistics. How are the men and horses to be fed, the vehicles fuelled? Supplies may take months to build up (six months in the case of the first Gulf War in 1991), and the 'umbilical cord of supply' must then be maintained. If the cord is cut, an army withers and dies. Alexander, for instance, covered the very region Genghis was now about to enter. To ensure his columns travelled only with essentials, Alexander burned his own treasure-wagon, then ordered his officers to do the same. But he still had to establish forward supply bases for his foot soldiers.

Genghis had no such problems. His horse-borne army had no need of an umbilical cord or forward supply bases. Its fuel was grass, which ran like an open pipeline from Mongolia all the way to Hungary (as he would later discover). Horses turn grass to meat and milk. On these simple products his men could survive for weeks, sleeping ten at a time in small cloth tents (*maikhan*). With oxen and camels loaded with *gers*, the army could even wait out a winter, killing cattle and eating dried meat. There were other requirements – an occasional boost from local produce, a source of wood to make arrows, iron for the smiths to make arrowheads – but in essence this was like a whole army of special forces: self-reliant, independent, a tribe of soldiers ready for action for years at a time.

Even so, taking city after city would be a slow job, if the Mongols had nothing but siege machinery to help them. But they had in addition one other weapon that had been brought to a high level in China: terror, imposed in a very public way, so that all would observe and take note. Not only would the countryside be devastated by the field army of horsemen; not only would prisoners be used to push siege engines and fill in moats; but ruthlessness at this level would spread the word that the Mongols were invincible. Few cities would risk inevitable death by resisting, and most would surrender, preferring to be living slaves rather than corpses.

And his army would grow. With every city taken, it would be strengthened in wealth, numbers and weapons. Given one initial success – as Genghis knew from the China campaign – it would roll on, snowballing, limited only by geography, climate and the agenda of its supreme commander. No one at the time foresaw limits. True, Genghis's war aims were limited: to redress wrongs, acquire booty to pay his troops, and guarantee his new nation's security. But there was already a longer-term agenda implied by the backing of Eternal Heaven: today Khorazm, tomorrow China, and then the world, though the Mongols could have had no idea what that meant.

An account of Genghis's campaign against Khorazm should be required reading for all students of military history. Unfortunately, it doesn't exist. *The Secret History* is so obsessed by its domestic story that military matters are omitted, or left vague, or totally muddled. Muslim sources are concerned with death and destruction on their own side. Genghis's genius as a strategist emerges only as a shadow-show.

The first thing the campaign reveals is his skill at choosing his commanders. He was no Hitler, ready to browbeat subordinates, convinced of his own abilities. Jebe, who had saved his life by sucking poison from a wound, and Subodei, who had 'drunk the muddy waters of Baljuna' – these were the two he relied on most.

Genghis and Subodei, together with Genghis's sons Jochi and Chagadai as nominal commanders-in-chief, gathered the army – actually three separate forces – together in the grasslands of Kazakhstan just south and east of Lake Balkash in the summer of 1219. Having already crossed some 2,000 kilometres, the army needed rest. The troops were there for three months, gathering strength, fattening their horses. Now, 150,000 men and perhaps half a million horses would have been rather obvious. So would their purpose: to follow the grasslands westwards in parallel to the mountain ranges that are part of the Hindu Kush–Tien Shan massifs, swing round the spur of the Karatau mountains, hit the Syr Darya river and head south into Khorazm's heartland at the base of the rich Fergana valley. There really was no other route, as Mohammed knew from his spies, for their way south was blocked by mountains, and further west were the formidable wastes of the Kyzylkum desert.

Mohammed should have concentrated his forces and used them to attack. But he couldn't, because he had no faith in his generals. Fearing they would either scrap with each other or combine against him, he created a defence line spread out in fortresses along the Syr Darya river.

That was just what Genghis wanted, because the obvious strategy was not the only one. Some 650 kilometres to the south, the other side of the mountains in the heart of what had until recently been Kara Khitai, was Jebe, with 20,000 men. He led them through the mountains and down the Fergana valley, heading for precisely the spot Mohammed thought Genghis would be

## GENGHIS'S LEADERSHIP SECRETS NOS 15–17

# SURPRISE + TERROR + MAGNANIMATY = VICTORY

The campaign against Khorazm in 1219 reveals strategic brilliance seldom matched in military history. Ideally, Genghis would have attacked with overwhelming force, as the United States did in Iraq in 2004. But this was not an option. In numbers and technology, the two sides were evenly matched. Moreover, Mohammed had the advantage of fighting on his home ground, while Genghis's army had to carry his siege weapons over 3,000 kilometres, in theory giving Mohammed time enough to prepare formidable defences. The Mongols, however, had advantages of their own. One was the weakness of Mohammed's leadership. Another was that the Mongols' fuel – grass – was supplied by nature. But these alone did not guarantee success. To ensure victory, Genghis had to work in three other elements. The first was surprise, made possible by the formidable skill and toughness of Mongol cavalry. This would allow not one but two outflanking manoeuvres. The second was ruthless commitment to the task in hand. The Mongols used terror as a strategy, acting with such appalling brutality in one city that others simply surrendered. Third, to be appealing, surrender had to be seen to be of benefit: people had to understand that if opposition meant death, then surrender meant survival. Genghis could not afford to indulge in racial or religious prejudice. Genocide would not work.

homing in on: except he came from the east, unannounced, bypassing the shah's defensive line and aiming for the great cities of Samarkand and Bukhara. Quickly, the shah redeployed some of the Syr Darya forces to defend the cities.

At the same time, Genghis, with Subodei as his chief of staff, set out to attack the other end of the Syr Darya line. First stop: Otrar, where the trouble had started. Genghis wanted the governor taken alive, to ensure him a painful end. The siege lasted for five months – a reminder that siege engines did not guarantee rapid victory – until the Mongols forced an entry. Inalchuk met a lingering death, and the city was flattened. On went two armies, under Jochi and Chagadai, to take on the vulnerable units scattered along the Syr Darya line, which was now being threatened from both left and right. For a month, the Mongol pincers chewed at the shah's flanks.

What, meanwhile, of Genghis? After Otrar – perhaps even while the siege was still going on – he had vanished. Unseen by any spies, he was doing the impossible: with the third army of 40,000 (in very round figures) he struck out southward across the Kyzylkum desert, 450 kilometres of bitter, sand-and-tussock wilderness. Impossible? Not at all. The distance involved was half the distance between his old headquarters in Mongolia and Beijing, and the conditions were about the same as the worst bits of the Gobi. He had done a forced march like this several times. It was so routine that no Gobi crossing rates a mention in *The Secret History*. Mongol soldiers could carry five days' supplies. They had locals with them to point out the occasional water-holes, where desert nomads raised sheep, camels and horses. What was impossible to the shah was second nature to Genghis. He appeared out of the void at the far end of Mohammed's defensive line, and proceeded to 'roll it up', in military terminology.

As the Mongol army approached Bukhara in February or March 1220, the townspeople, unwilling to be killed for the sake of a ruler they despised, opened the gates. Genghis rode in, through alleys lined with the wooden houses of the common people, past palaces of baked-earth brick, into the inner city, the Shahristan, to the city's largest building. He thus found himself master of one of the richest cities in one of the most sophisticated cultures on earth.

Juvaini records what happened next in vivid detail. Genghis entered the main mosque, where he uttered infamous words: 'The countryside is empty of fodder; fill our horses' bellies.' While the horrified imams and other notables held the Mongols' horses, troops emptied grain stores, tossing Qurans from their wooden cases to make feeding-troughs. This was probably not deliberate desecration, more unheeding practicality. But there was a lesson to be drawn, as Genghis saw instantly. Here was evidence of Heaven's backing. In the *musalla*, a courtyard for prayers during festivals held outside the city walls, he summoned a carefully selected audience of 280 men. He mounted the pulpit, and gave them his explanation for his rise and their fall:

> O people, know that you have committed great sins, and that the great ones among you have committed these sins. If you ask me what proof I have for these words, I say it is because I am the punishment of God. If you had not committed great sins, God would not have sent a punishment like me upon you.

Did this really happen? Not unless Genghis had suddenly learned Persian. Perhaps there was an interpreter. Or perhaps the story is apocryphal. Anyway, it has become part of folklore, because it fitted the circumstances well, given Khorazm's appalling leadership and the way Muslims had torn their own society apart over recent decades. The punishment his audience now received was to be robbed. Each was given a guard to ensure they were robbed only by Genghis or his generals, not by ordinary troopers. For the next few days, with the sultan's soldiers and their families penned in the citadel and the towns-people cowed in their houses, the rich and their escorts filed out of the city to Genghis's tent, where they handed over their cash, jewellery, clothing and fabrics.

After that came the destruction of the citadel and the disposal of the population. Defenders were killed in action or executed, including all males 'who stood higher than the butt of a whip'. The surviving citizens were herded together in the *musalla* to be distributed, the young men into military service, women into slavery with their children, the blacksmiths, carpenters and gold-workers to teams of Mongol artisans.

Then the Mongol juggernaut rolled on east towards Samarkand, the new capital, defended by between 40,000 and 110,000 troops (or perhaps that was the number of people; the sources vary hugely), sheltering inside a moat, and city walls, and a citadel, all hastily strengthened in the weeks since the siege of Otrar had begun. Driving crowds of prisoners ahead of them, the Mongols set up camp right around the town. Mohammed fled, urging everyone along his route to gather their goods and get out because resistance was useless – not exactly an act to boost morale. The merchant princes and clerics of Samarkand, unprepared to risk death for such a man, sued for peace, and received similar treatment to the inhabitants of Bukhara, with Mongol commanders and their families taking their pick of possessions, women and artisans.

Khorazm's *coup de grâce* would, of course, include the capture or death of the fleeing Mohammed, a task given to Jebe and Subodei, who hounded him across present-day Uzbekistan, Turkmenistan and Iran, to the Caspian. There he and a small retinue rowed to an island, where he died of shock and despair.

The speed of the advance and its impact on the cowed people suggested an idea to Jebe and Subodei: if the world was to fall to the Mongols, the sooner they found out what they were up against the better. Genghis agreed: further evidence of the total trust he had in his companions. And what a way to maintain the momentum of this astonishing advance, and also sustain the morale of these shock troops. Baghdad would not fall easily. But to the north lay another world: the Caucasus, and Russia, with what beyond? The decision inspired one of the most extraordinary adventures in military history, a 7,500-kilometre, two-year gallop through Georgia across southern Russia to the Black Sea, up the Volga, then back to rejoin Genghis as he returned from Khorazm. This – the Great Raid, as it has become known – was perhaps the highest-risk, most rewarding reconnaissance in history. With some 20,000 men and some 80,000 horses, the two generals explored the grass-lands of southern Russia and discovered they could defeat the disunited, cumbersome Russian armies. Not only were they fuelled by grass all the way, they financed themselves by robbing every tribe and culture they met. They also picked up information about what lay further west: the rich cities of Russia, more grassland – fuel for their horses, enough perhaps to take Genghis's empire all the way across the continent, into Hungary, and then to who knew what cities in Europe. By the time they rejoined Genghis, they were both rich and extremely well informed, with all the information Genghis's heirs would need for the invasion of Russia and eastern Europe 20 years later.

## The killing fields of Khorazm

Meanwhile, the Mongol pincers closed on the remaining great city of Khorazm: Gurganj, or Urgench as it later became (and still is). It refused to surrender. Here, in the flood plain of the Amu Darya, there were no stones for the catapults, so the Mongols cut up mulberry trees to make ammunition. Prisoners, as usual, were forced to fill in the moats and then undermine the walls. With the walls down, the Mongols fought street by street to victory. The women and those captives with any skill, 100,000 of them, were taken into slavery; the rest were led away to slaughter. Juvaini speaks of 50,000 soldiers killing 24 men each. That makes *1.2 million* dead.

Finally, Genghis designated Tolui to complete the conquest of the western regions, beyond the Amu Darya. In three months, he dealt with the three main cities of Merv, Nishapur and Herat. Nishapur fell in April: its people were killed, the town razed and ploughed over in revenge for the loss of one of Genghis's sons-in-law to a Muslim arrow. Herat wisely surrendered, and most of its people were spared. In Merv, though, 60 captured Mongols were

paraded through the town and then executed, a humiliation which, when Genghis and Tolui heard of it, ensured
a terrible fate for all within its walls. Just 7,000 Mongols
laid siege to the city, defended by an army of 12,000 and a
population swollen to over ten times its normal level of
about 70,000 by refugees from the surrounding villages.
But there was no escape, and fear trumped bravery. After
a week, the city sued for peace. The Mongols entered the
city, unopposed. For four days they drove the docile crowds
out on to the plain, taking care to separate out 400 crafts-
men and a crowd of children to act as slaves. Then the
killing started. 'To each man was allotted the execution of
three or four hundred persons.' Then, when the Mongols
departed, came the reckoning, conducted by a team under
an eminent cleric. It took them two weeks, at the end of
which they concluded, 'Taking into account only those that
were plain to see and leaving aside those that had been
killed in holes and cavities and in the villages and deserts,
they arrive at a figure of more than one million three
hundred thousand.'

Another 1.3 million? And this in addition to the 1.2
million supposedly killed in Urgench? It sounds incredible.
But we know from recent horrors – Armenia, the
Holocaust, Rwanda – that mass slaughter comes easily to
those with the will, leadership and technology. It's more
than possible to kill 1.3 million, and in hours. For a
Mongol, an unresisting prisoner would have been as easy
to despatch as a sheep, and of far less value. Seven
thousand men could have slaughtered a million in the
course of a single morning.

This was undoubtedly slaughter on an unprecedented
scale. Even supposing the figures were exaggerated, we

have to assume that something like 25 per cent of a population of 5 million died – 1.25 million deaths in three years. This was an appalling blow for a rich and sophisticated urban society, but less than totally destructive: it left enough for life to recover with the passing of the years.

This was not a Holocaust or a genocide, because it was the consequence not of state policy applied to a whole culture or people, but of strategy. It saves so much trouble and expense if cities capitulate without a struggle, so every city was offered a choice: give up, or die. Granted, non-Mongols were considered inferior, but they could always choose to concede the 'truth' of Mongol supremacy, and then be free to serve, if only as concubines and slaves; but then, with time and talent, the women might produce worthy sons and gain influence; and the men might have a chance to rise to high office, as at least two had done before Genghis became khan, and others would do later. The Khorazmian massacres were the cumulative effect of one-off applications of a decision to use terror for strategic purposes, a strategy that deserves its own term: urbicide.

Strategically, Genghis's ruthlessness was the consequence of military necessity, and displayed brilliance of a high order. He could not afford to go into Khorazm without two vital elements: rapid victory and an exit strategy. The first, rapid victory, had been handed to him by Mohammed: a ruler who had managed to alienate his own subjects, and thus guaranteed a weak response and a lack of resistance. As for the second, the brutal tactic to take cities – surrender, or die – was the *coup de grâce* that brought a quick end to the war. With victory secured, the Mongols could embark on the wider strategy: administration, control, and the withdrawal of many troops.

There would be no quagmire here, no wishful thinking, no squandering of resources. It was all over in eighteen months.

Well, almost. Mohammed's heroic son, Jalal ad-Din, rallied some surviving forces and retreated southward, into present-day Afghanistan, pursued by Genghis. In the spring of 1221, at Parvan, just north of Kabul, he inflicted the first defeat the Mongols had suffered in the whole of this campaign. But it was only a temporary reversal. Jalal retreated through the Hindu Kush to northern India's stifling plains, until he was trapped between the Indus and the advancing Mongols. This was the end for his army, but not for Jalal, who forced his horse into the water and reached safety on the far bank. Watching in astonishment and admiration, Genghis let him go, saying, 'Every father should have such a son!' Jalal lived on until his unrecorded death, possibly at the hands of Kurdish robbers, a few years later.

Rather oddly, the limit of Genghis's advance in late 1221 nearly coincided with the limit of Alexander's some 1500 years earlier. Alexander stopped because his army refused to go any further. Perhaps Genghis came under the same pressure. One story told in several sources claims that Genghis was put off advancing further by meeting a one-horned animal – possibly a rhinoceros, a creature not yet extinct in north-west India – that spoke to his guards, saying, 'Your Lord should return home immediately!' Could the sighting have given a nervous officer a diplomatic cover to pass on the feelings of his mutinous troops? Perhaps this was the excuse Genghis himself needed to consolidate his gains and turn back from an adventure that was, at last, too big for him.

# 6

# SAGE:
# THE SEARCH FOR
# ULTIMATE TRUTHS

REWIND THREE years, to 1218, when Genghis recruited Chucai. Much of north China was his, the rest would follow, and presumably so would the south, Song itself, in due course. He did not yet know that his plans were about to be disrupted by grisly developments in Otrar. In odd moments, he had time to ponder. Was this all there was to life? Conquest, death and destruction, more conquest? What did it all mean?

Genghis was the instrument through which the will of Blue Heaven, or Eternal Heaven, or God, was being fulfilled, as proved by the success of his campaigns. Throughout the histories of the major religions, theologians have agonized about how to recognize God's will. Genghis endured no such agonies, because his successes made God's will manifest: a nation and a region had already been given to the Mongols. It was merely a question now of finding out the extent of the gift. The whole world, perhaps? That was certainly what Genghis's heirs came to believe. However great its extent, it was the will of Heaven, and the Mongols' task was to have everyone acknowledge this astonishing fact. As Güyük wrote to the pope nineteen years after Genghis's death: 'How can anybody achieve anything except on God's order?' Yes, other major religions offered different paths to the same

Heaven. But the plain fact was, as any Mongol would have argued, that Heaven favoured the Mongols.

On the other hand stood the uncertainty about the nature of the godhead – not so much *what* had been granted, but *by what?* What was the nature of this godhead? Other mysteries remained to be solved: like *why?* And what obligations did that gift impose? It must have been puzzling to be snatched from obscurity, and protected, and rewarded for his obedience with unprecedented conquests, and yet granted no insight into the nature of the universe. Genghis was open to anyone who might offer guidance.

*Genghis was open to anyone who might offer guidance.*

There were several ways he might have gone about addressing the questions that bothered him. Shamanism he had tried, and found wanting. Success had come so fast that there had been no time to develop a cult that might have been able to question Eternal Heaven. Nestorian Christianity, the faith adopted by his 'father' Toghril, was a minor sect of a distant religion, and hadn't done Toghril much good; of Islam he knew nothing, yet; and what could the Chinese offer, those effete, land-grubbing, luxury-weakened city-dwellers?

As it happened, he was about to find out, for he had just employed one of China's most gifted men, Yelü Chucai. Though employed as an administrator, Chucai also happened to be both a highly original scholar and a man with a mission. He was dedicated to the idea that his new master, Genghis, had been chosen by Heaven, and that it was therefore Chucai's Heaven-directed brief to help Genghis's transformation from barbarian warlord to universal emperor. This was his stated agenda. As he

GENGHIS'S LEADERSHIP SECRET NO. 18

## PHILOSOPHIZE (OR AT LEAST PRETEND TO)

One of Genghis's most unexpected traits was his intellectual curiosity. He was illiterate and, as far as is known, uneducated. Yet he had a deep interest in religion, inspired by his own success, which he believed was achieved with the support of Heaven. Why was this so? What response did it call for? He had no answers. But his openness unwittingly joined him to an ancient debate that ran across many cultures: should a ruler also be a philosopher? Or should he rely on advisers? Chinese scholars believed rulers should rely on advice. In the fifth and fourth centuries BC, Plato argued that kings should be 'genuine and adequate philosophers', whereas his pupil Aristotle argued that kings 'should take advice from true philosophers'. In the ninth and tenth centuries AD, the Islamic philosopher al-Farabi argued that theology, lawgiving, philosophy and kingship must all combine to underpin society. Genghis learned of such matters from his scholarly adviser Yelü Chucai, who determined to make Genghis into a Daoist sage. Genghis responded, or seemed to. Whatever his real beliefs, Genghis apparently saw the advantages of being seen as a thoughtful ruler committed to austerity, selfless service and the welfare of his people.

wrote in his *Record of a Journey to the West*: 'I wished to make Our Sovereign [Genghis] tread loftily in the footsteps of the ancient worthies.'[1] On the basis of Chucai's

---

[1] Quoted in de Rachewiltz, 'Yeh-lü Ch'u-ts'ai, Yeh-lü Chu, Yeh-lü Hsi-liang', in *In the Service of the Khan*.

interests and Genghis's later actions, it is possible to speculate about what Chucai might have told his new master to bring about this change.

On his retreat in the three years after the fall of Beijing, Chucai had cut himself off from friends and family and become the disciple of a monk named Wansong. During this time, Chucai would have immersed himself in the classics, which included ancient works on warfare, administration and leadership. Genghis would surely have been impatient with much of the philosophy and ritual to which his new adviser introduced him, time being short, but Chucai would have been eager to explore a few fundamental precepts: that only political unity can bring wars to a lasting end; that good rule must begin in the heart and mind of the ruler.

No doubt the first advice related to the most urgent matter, the invasion of Khorazm; hence (possibly) the introduction of Genghis to Sun Zi. To this exposition Chucai would have added other advice on the business of leadership and its essential qualities: wisdom, sincerity, benevolence, courage and strictness. He would have pointed out that Sun Zi drew on even more ancient classics, the *Yi Jing* (*I Ching, The Book of Changes*) and the *Dao De Jing* (*Tao Te Ching / The Way and its Power*), with their insistence on austerity – 'Cut off one well-spring, that of profiteering, and that is ten times better than mobilizing an army' – and hatred of violence:

*Those who enjoy killing people*
*Cannot get their will in the world.*

He would have spoken of Kong Fuzi – Confucius, as he is known in the West – the sixth-century BC sage whose system of ethics and government is founded on the principle that through the exercise of loyalty, piety, filial respect and benevolence all will be well, for leaders and followers alike. But all was not always well, as the countless wars and endless deaths endured by the Warring States (475–221 BC) testified. Another philosophy arose, known as Legalism, which advised rulers to adopt the most extreme, fascistic, Machiavellian policies to exercise power. Chucai would have pointed to Legalism's most brilliant exponent, the First Emperor, who unified China in 221 BC. He would also have pointed out that the First Emperor's dynasty was China's shortest, lasting a mere fifteen years. Extreme oppression aroused extreme opposition. Here too was a lesson: better to rely on other qualities – the ancient virtues of Daoism, or some of them, such as frugality, courage and generosity, and its ancient objectives, such as health, wealth and longevity, perhaps even immortality. Daoism had become intertwined with Buddhism, but shortly before Genghis's rise a new Daoist sect had arisen: known as Complete Perfection, it promoted the belief, shared by Chucai's master Wansong and Chucai himself, that the 'Three Teachings' of Buddhism, Confucianism and Daoism were at heart all one. It was this sect and its leader Changchun that Chucai recommended to Genghis, who must surely have been intrigued to find such eminent scholars supporting his own belief that the old nomad virtues of austerity and generosity were rather more effective than brutality.

# Talking of immortality

After a few lessons along these lines, it may well have seemed to Chucai that Genghis was beginning to acquire the attributes of a Daoist adept. It was time to consolidate progress.

Then or soon afterwards, while Genghis was preparing to advance westward into Khorazm, Chucai pointed out that in fact Changchun was the man who could take Genghis further along this road. Politically, he would be useful, because he exercised a benign influence over Genghis's new and restive Chinese subjects. It was the practical potential of alchemy that clinched matters. Genghis was now getting on for 60, and could not go on campaigning for ever. Changchun, so it was said, was 300 years old, and could teach the secret of his longevity. Off went an invitation across the Central Asian grasslands, the Gobi and the war-torn countryside of north China to Changchun's temple 500 kilometres from Beijing, on the Shandong peninsula.

The invitation was written in classical Chinese style, as if from a Daoist monk and austere warrior, not from a conqueror who could, if he wished, lay claim to the wealth of much of north China:

> Heaven has abandoned China owing to its haughtiness and extravagant luxury. But I, living in the northern wilderness, have not inordinate passions. I hate luxury and exercise moderation. I have only one coat and one food. I eat the same food and am dressed in the same tatters as my humble herdsmen. I consider the people my children, and take an

interest in talented men as if they were my brothers
... At military exercises I am always in the front,
and in time of battle am never behind. In the
space of seven years I have succeeded in accomplish-
ing a great work, and uniting the whole world
in one empire. I have not myself distinguishing
qualities.[2]

This is a remarkable statement, so important that it
was transcribed on to stone. The words may be Chucai's –
probably were, since they were in Chinese – but Genghis
surely agreed with the sentiments: that a leader should be
the epitome of personal virtue, living simply, sharing the
suffering of ordinary people, caring for others (as long as
the 'others' were Mongols, of course).

Changchun, though not 300, was still over 70, and tried
to make excuses. Other rulers had asked him to come to
court, but he had refused. This time no refusal was
possible. Clearly, it was the will of Heaven. 'I have grown
old, and am not yet dead,' he replied. 'But now, at the first
call of the Dragon Court, I am ready.' The old monk set off
on a journey that would cover 10,000 kilometres and take
almost four years, as his disciple Li Zhichang recorded in
one of the most charming of travel books, *Journey to the
West*.[3]

This was the first time it had been possible for anyone,
let alone an elderly monk, to travel across Asia under the
protection of a single authority. Changchun's journey is

[2] Trans. Bretschneider, *Mediaeval Researches*, vol. 1.
[3] Not to be confused either with the famous sixteenth-century novel of the same name or
with Chucai's book. Li's has been translated into English twice, by Bretschneider and
Waley. See bibliography.

the first demonstration of the unprecedented freedom established by the Mongols over the previous 20 years. The Pax Mongolica would make it possible for numerous western travellers to cross Eurasia from west to east over the next 150 years – Christian priests, merchants and explorers, the most famous being Marco Polo. But the first to make the crossing came in the other direction, at the invitation of Genghis himself, who was by now deep in Afghanistan.

In the second week of May 1222, with the heat of early summer beginning to warm the Afghan highlands, the Master and the Khan met at last, speaking through an interpreter. It's hard to say who was most in awe of the other, the master of this world or that of the next. They greeted each other simply, bowing with hands together.

'Other rulers summoned you, but you would not go to them,' said Genghis (in Arthur Waley's translation). 'And now you have come 10,000 *li* to see me. I take this as a high compliment.'

The Master, describing himself as a mere hermit of the mountains, replied that the meeting was Heaven's will. Then Genghis came right to the point:

'Adept,' he asked, 'what Medicine of Long Life have you brought me from afar?'

'I have means of protecting life,' replied the Master, 'but no elixir that will prolong it.'

Far from being upset by the collapse of his expectations, Genghis 'was pleased with his candour' and was ready for the main purpose of the trip, as conceived by Chucai: namely, to receive from the Holy Immortal, as Genghis called him, instruction on good living and good ruling. But these regions were still not properly tamed.

There were still bandits in the mountains, and it would take months to quell them. The Master said that in that case it would be best for him to return to Samarkand. It was only a three-week journey there and back, nothing to one who had already travelled 10,000 *li*.

Back in Samarkand that summer, the city's governor made sure the Master lived well, in a house with a verandah that caught soft breezes, a bathing-place in a lake, and a garden which grew watermelons. In September came the return trip into Afghanistan, culminating in a discourse by Changchun on the Dao, the Way that underpins all things in Heaven and Earth. On 20 November 1222 Genghis had the Master's words recorded in Mongol and Chinese: When Man was first born, he shone with a holy radiance and his step was light. But his appetite and longing were so keen that his body grew heavy, his holy light dim, his life essence unbalanced. Those who study Dao seek to regain that balance by quietism, asceticism and meditation. In this lay the true elixir of long life. The khan should curb his appetites, live without desire, reject luscious tastes, eat only foods that are fresh and light, and abstain from lust. Try sleeping alone for a month, he advised. Genghis would be surprised what it would do for his energy level.

During the journey back to Mongolia, on which Changchun accompanied Genghis, the lessons continued, with a few more stern teachings: 'It is said that of the 3,000 sins the worst is ill-treatment of one's father and mother. Now in this respect I believe your subjects to be gravely at fault, and it would be well if your Majesty could use his influence to reform them.'

The khan was pleased: 'Holy Immortal, your words are

exceedingly true. Such is indeed my own belief.' Then to his ministers and officers he said: 'Heaven sent this Holy Immortal to tell me these things. Do you engrave them upon your hearts.' Perhaps they did; but they did not set them down on paper. The monk and his teachings get not a single mention in *The Secret History*, one of the few occasions on which its editor apparently ignored his master's voice. Perhaps he considered Genghis's interests to be out of character, or unhelpful to the imperial agenda. Or perhaps he knew Genghis's *real* opinion. Genghis was experimenting with the new entity he had created, which spanned two worlds, the nomadic and the settled, herder and farmer, Mongolian and Chinese. He may well have shown great respect for the Holy Immortal, yet also reserved judgement. He needed the old man's support, for political reasons. But what would be left of his appeal – his charisma – if he retreated into an inner world of peace and serenity?

Everyone came out ahead. Genghis ordered that Changchun and his disciples should be free from tax. On the monk's return to China, tax relief had a wonderful effect on his sect's income and recruitment. The Master urged his followers to accept Mongol rule with equanimity. From being a small sect, dominated by its parent and rival Buddhism, Daoism boomed, its growing bands of disciples taking over decaying Buddhist temples and building new ones.

# Beyond charisma to humility

So there's no denying that the summons, the meeting and the rewards had a political agenda, which suited both its *éminence grise*, Chucai, and Genghis himself. But I don't believe Genghis's respect was faked. He was no hypocrite. There was no denying either that Heaven was with him or that its nature was a mystery. Why was it that he, a minor impoverished aristocrat in a remote corner of a backwater, should be the recipient of such a gift? He could not understand, never would understand, and decided he had nothing to say on the matter. Not for him, therefore, the arrogance of an Alexander or an Augustus, who had themselves deified. Between divinity and his ignorant humanity a great gulf lay. These realizations created in Genghis a sense of humility, a very odd trait in a world conqueror.

Yet absolutely appropriate in a top leader, as Jim Collins writes in *Good to Great*, his book on what separates a great company from a merely good one. Having made detailed comparisons between the two, he and his team concluded that charismatic leadership is fine as far as it goes, but it has its dangers. His words are worth quoting, because they are so counter-intuitive. He is referring to corporate leaders, but the conclusion applies with equal force to leaders in other fields:

> Strong, charismatic leaders . . . can all too easily become the de facto reality driving a company. Throughout the study, we found comparison companies where the top leader led with such force or instilled such fear that people worried more about the leader – what he would say, what he would think, what he would do – than they worried about external reality and what *it* could do to the company . . . The moment a leader allows himself to become the primary reality people worry about, rather than

reality being the primary reality, you have a recipe for mediocrity, or worse. This is one of the key reasons why less charismatic leaders often produce better long-term results than their more charismatic counterparts. Indeed for those of you with a strong, charismatic personality, it is worthwhile to consider the idea that charisma can be as much a liability as an asset.

History offers many examples of leaders who confused cause and personality, and sacrificed the one to the other: in our own time, Mugabe and Saddam come to mind. Not so Genghis, who looked beyond his own personality to an enduring empire. His decision – or rather his decision to accept Chucai's advice – to summon Changchun has a parallel in the practice of those Roman emperors who, during victory parades, had a mentor alongside them in the chariot, muttering reminders of the ruler's mortality.

Yet despite the grandeur of this aim, the nature of his faith – certainty combined with ignorance – suggested the need for toleration that is recorded in one of the Yasa's statements: 'He ordered that all religions were to be respected and that no preference was to be shown to any of them. All this he commanded in order that it might be agreeable to God.' This attitude wove itself into the imperial administration after his death. When a French envoy, William, from Rubrouck in north-eastern France, met Genghis's grandson Mönkhe in 1254, the khan told him: 'We Mongols believe that there is only one God through whom we have life and through whom we die . . . But just as God has given the hand several fingers, so he has given mankind several paths,' namely the major

GENGHIS'S LEADERSHIP SECRET NO. 19

## CULTIVATE HUMILITY

In this respect Genghis was in tune with modern leadership theory. In *Good to Great*, Jim Collins argues that leaders fall into one of five categories: Highly Capable Individual, Contributing Team Member, Competent Manager, Effective Leader and Level 5 Executive. It's the last one we're interested in here. Level 5 leaders are those dedicated not to the cult of their own personality but to the cause, whatever its nature. Such a leader is 'an individual who blends extreme personal humility with intense professional will . . . Level 5 leaders channel their ego needs away from themselves and into the larger goal of building a great company. It's not that Level 5 leaders have no ego or self-interest. Indeed, they are incredibly ambitious – *but their ambition is first and foremost for the institution, not themselves.*'

religions – Buddhism, Daoism, Islam and Christianity, all of which were represented at his court.

Humility and tolerance together: two surprising traits in a world conqueror notorious for his power and brutality. Their coexistence explains something else about him, which may be seen as either a limitation or a virtue, or even both.

Once when I was arguing for this idea in a Malaysian university, an earnest young lady in a headscarf stood up and asked if I was really claiming that Genghis was greater than Mohammed. The question made me pause, not only because, as I recalled with a sudden onset of nerves, I was in a community and a nation of Muslims; it was an interesting comparison. Mohammed, like Genghis, was born of poor nomadic pastoralists into a feuding culture in a harsh land. He was soon orphaned. He too had a vision of unity under God. But he was a lot closer to his God than Genghis was, and he heard a voice telling him to 'Recite, in the name of the Lord, who created / Created man from a clot of blood.' He too believed himself to be chosen, as God's mouthpiece. After 22 years of contemplation and 'recitation', he inspired one of the great formative books, the Quran, which, as well as communicating his passionate vision of godly life, also crystallized his language. Like Genghis, he placed blood second to his belief, his vision. He, like Genghis, was concerned with creating a community, delivering guidance on food, marriage and war. He was both prophet and sovereign, and on his death he left a new religion that was carried by the sword in a swirl of fervour, political rivalry and desire for plunder. The result was an empire unified only by faith and the holy book – very different from Genghis's, which was created as a political entity first and foremost.

Perhaps comparisons between two such different empires are odious; but one difference stands out: Genghis invented nothing new in religious terms, and did not inspire his own people to heights of literary creativity (*The Secret History*, important though it is, does not compare with the Quran, any more than with the Bible or the works of Homer.) Genghis's aim, and his heirs' aim, was to sustain political dominance by resolving religious differences, not to create new ones. Mongols have been unified by admiration for Genghis; but this is hardly to be compared to adoration of a prophet revered as the mouthpiece of God. In the end, he had no great message for humanity. The Mongol empire had no greater cause than its own existence.

This is a limitation, if you think that greatness in leadership must include religious creativity. Personally, I think the world should be grateful for the limitation. Think what further disasters – the conversions under duress, the gruesome martyrdoms, the eccentric rituals, the purges, the ever more brutal conquests, the sectarian disputes – might have been imposed if Genghis had founded a church, commissioned priests to dream up a theology, and forced that faith upon his unwilling subjects. With that as a legacy, perhaps the Mongols would not have been so ready to retreat from Hungary in 1242. In this respect, we all had a lucky escape.

# 7

# CONSPIRATOR:
# THE LAST CAMPAIGN
# AND DEATH

WHEN GENGHIS arrived back in Mongolia early in 1225, it was to prepare for war against his faithless vassal Xi Xia. A year later he was ready, his army restored by a summer's grazing and fortified with several thousand troops from Khorazm and other non-Mongol tribes. His war aim was, as always, to take the rest of Jin, only half of which had been conquered. Xi Xia had to fall first, to stop it coming to the help of the principal target.

Once again he led his army across the Gobi to an area rich in herds of wild asses. Genghis, as active as ever in his mid-sixties, was not one to miss a chance like that. But during an ass-hunt he fell from his horse and injured himself so badly that his generals advised withdrawal.[1]

Typically, he refused. 'The Tangut people will say that we turned back because we lost heart,' he said: a bold decision, for it meant spending the winter in the field. Hoping to get his way without an invasion, he sent a message offering a peaceful solution – in return, of course, for full compliance. But the Tanguts' general, Asha, was adamant. He had an encampment in the Helan mountains,

---

[1] It is said by some that the fall was the cause of his death. Yet he remained campaigning for more than a year, so it couldn't have been fatal.

he said: 'Let us fight there!' When the reply came, Genghis, now on his way to recovery, was incensed. 'How can one withdraw? Even if we die, let us challenge their boasts,' he said, and placed himself in the hands of his god: 'Eternal Heaven, you be the judge!'

His decision was made easier by Asha's rebuff, which implied the strategy that he expected the Mongols to follow: a fast sweep south-east, along the same route they had taken in the first invasion, and a good clean fight in the Xi Xia backyard, where the Tanguts could draw on their two main cities, Yinchuan and Wuwei, for reserves. Genghis, therefore, would do the exact opposite, adopting the strategy he had used in Khorazm: a swift advance south-*west*, through the back door, circling around the desert and approaching the enemy's heartland along the Yellow River.

When spring came, Genghis was well enough to lead his army for two or three hard days across the 250 kilometres of sand and gravel that separate the Three Beauties from Xi Xia's northern stronghold, the city the Mongols knew as Khara-Khoto, the Black City. Guarding a grim landscape of gravel deserts, it was a thriving outpost of perhaps several thousand people. Here there was water, in the form of lakes where a river, the Etsin (the Ruo / 弱 in Chinese), flows down from the Qilian mountains to the south.

No army came to meet the invaders. Khara-Khoto didn't stand a chance. Now the Mongols could as usual draw on prisoners, defectors, supplies and weapons to take the next city, by negotiation if possible, by force if necessary. As in Khorazm, this was no blitzkrieg, but a steady advance that fuelled itself, progressing with the momentum of a slow-motion avalanche.

Two months later and 250 kilometres further south, at the Qilian mountains, Genghis could afford to divide his growing army. A subsidiary force under Subodei headed west to take the most distant cities of the realm, while the main army struck east towards the heart of Xi Xia.

In autumn 1226 Genghis, returning from a summer break in the Qilian mountains, rejoined his army at the Yellow River and crossed the great watercourse, possibly using sheepskin or cowskin floats to carry platforms such as locals used to ship cargoes of grain and salt downriver. He then circled north, approaching Yinchuan from the south-east – a direction precisely opposite to the one Asha had proposed in his challenge.

His approach shattered Tangut morale. The ineffective emperor, Li Dewang, died, and the poisoned chalice of kingship fell to a kinsman, Li Xian, though his reign was so brief and what followed so destructive that he is virtually nothing but a wraith.

In December 1226 Genghis again divided his army into two. One force laid siege to Yinchuan, while the other under his personal command went off not only to secure other smaller cities to the east and south, but also in pursuit of the wider scheme against Jin. The purpose of this advance was to snip off a narrow tongue of western Jin, to prevent Jin troops coming to the rescue of their Tangut allies, and to prepare for the final conquest of Jin.

A few weeks later Genghis heard that, after six months of starvation and sickness, Li Xian was prepared to capitulate. All he needed, he said, was a month's grace to prepare suitable gifts, hoping for easy treatment and a long reign as a vassal. Genghis had no intention of granting either. But nor did he want to hint at his true purpose, which was, as always with those who resisted, and more so with this twice-treacherous people, to be utterly ruthless. No grounds for trust or reconciliation were left. They would be 'blown to the winds like hearth ashes'. As *The Secret History* grimly states, Genghis decreed: 'Kill the valiant, the bold, the manly and the fine Tanguts, and let the soldiers take for themselves as many of the common Tanguts as they can lay hands on and capture.' This was not the order of a Daoist, acting under Chucai's advice; and he was contemplating nothing so restrained as urbicide. Having made the mistake of trusting the Tangut leaders once, and having been betrayed by them twice, he was set on a punishment that sounds perilously close to genocide. As a first step in this dreadful process, the Tangut ruler had to die.

Now it was summer, some of which Genghis spent in the Liupan mountains before leading his main army on southward across the crucial tongue of Jin territory. One hundred kilometres south of the mountains, just short of the Jin–Song border, everything seemed about to fall into place. Genghis was right on the verge of the final conquest of Xi Xia and had just occupied part of western Jin, the base from which to complete the conquest of all north China, giving him an empire running from the Pacific almost to Baghdad. The emperor of Xi Xia was already on his way to capitulate. The work of a lifetime was about to pay off.

## The deathbed conspiracy

At this crucial moment, in early August 1227, Genghis fell ill, perhaps with the typhus brought by troops in their march southward. It was serious, and everyone near him knew it. It was impossible to hide the fact of his malady; but its gravity had to be kept secret. So, on the first day of the last week of his life, Genghis was rushed in a closed cart into a hidden, fertile valley in the Liupan mountains, where secrecy could be guaranteed. In 2000 this glorious place of steep forests divided by rushing streams was made a 6,000-square-kilometre national park, the Liupan Shan State Forest Park, with a new road leading to a campsite. It is still famous for its medicinal plants. I saw a list of 39 of them when I was there a few years ago. Here he could be given any number of remedies.

Nothing worked. But for a few days Genghis was still the strategist, planning for the future. In one version of these events, written by the Persian historian Rashid ad-Din a couple of generations later, Genghis said: 'Do not let my death be known. Do not weep or lament in any way, so that the enemy shall not know anything about it. But when the ruler of the Tanguts and the population leave the city at the appointed hour, annihilate them all.' So what followed was, I think, Genghis's last supreme effort to make sure that his Heaven-backed plan for universal rule did not falter, whatever his own fate.

First, as Chinese sources record, Genghis laid out the strategy by which Jin was to be defeated. To take the rest of Jin would mean taking the new capital, Kaifeng. To do that, the Mongols should first find a solution to the problem posed by a powerful fortress overlooking the narrow Tong pass, set between mountains and the junction of the Wei and Yellow Rivers. Ever since the time of the First Emperor in the third century BC, it had been the key to the lower Yellow River. Some 350 kilometres downstream lay

Kaifeng. Genghis knew what he was talking about: the Mongols had taken the fortress once before in 1216, only to lose it again when they retreated. It would now be too well defended to take. But both the Tong pass fortress and Kaifeng itself were near Jin's southern border with Song. Best therefore to get Song's permission to march around the Tong pass and approach Kaifeng from the south: 'Since Jin and Song have been enemies for generations, Song will certainly agree.' This would force the Jin to send reinforcements from the Tong pass fortress, both exhausting the troops and weakening the fortress, which could then be taken, leaving Kaifeng without its main defence. As it happened, this was exactly the plan of campaign that Genghis's successors used in their final defeat of Jin seven years later.

But this brilliant plan, indeed the empire itself, was set at risk by Genghis's illness. The emperor of Xi Xia, on his way from Yinchuan, might well have no one to surrender to. If he heard the news, he would return, and appeal to Jin. Xi Xia and Jin had been allies before. Yes, Jin had recently rejected his advances, but that was before the Mongols had taken the war into Jin territory. Now the two would be natural allies, joining forces against a common enemy, destroying Genghis's grand strategy.

There was only one possible course of action. Everything had to go forward as planned. No hint of the truth must leak out. It was vital, therefore, that the Xi Xia emperor arrive, capitulate,

*Everything had to go forward as planned.*

and then become the first of his treacherous people to die.

But the plot needed careful handling.[2] These were a religious people. One of Li Xian's honorifics was a Buddhist title, Iluhu Burkhan, Exalted Holy One. It would not be quite the thing to murder such an illustrious religious figure in cold blood. To reduce Li Xian into something expendable, Genghis gave him the title Shidurgu, *shudarga* in modern Mongolian, meaning 'loyal'. It seemed merely to confirm his imminent submission. In fact, it was a death sentence in disguise. He would certainly become a loyal vassal – after his death, when he would serve Genghis in the afterlife.

Where was Li Xian to submit? Certainly not in the secret base hidden in the mountains. It so happens that there was a suitable site on open ground close by. Between Guyuan and the Liupan Shan, in the low terraced hills near a village called Kaicheng, Genghis had decreed a temporary headquarters. This new HQ, with its tent-palaces and garrison, now found a second use, as a base for the meeting with the emperor of Xi Xia when he arrived to make his final capitulation.

This, like much else surrounding Genghis's death, is conjectural. But there is evidence. Decades later, Genghis's grandson Kublai, whose conquests went much further towards realizing Genghis's dreams, built this into a substantial provincial headquarters. One of Kublai's grandsons was based here in 1297, in charge of the area's defences with 10,000 troops. In 1306 an earthquake destroyed it, killing 5,000. The people fled, the baked-earth buildings were washed away, and it vanished from sight and memory.

---

[2] I told this story in *Genghis Khan: Life, Death and Resurrection*, but this version is updated because I have been able to draw on Igor de Rachewiltz's new version of *The Secret History*, with its detailed commentary; see bibliography.

Archaeologists are now beginning a huge research project to resurrect it. Why did Kublai choose it in the first place? Perhaps because Kaicheng was in effect a sacred site, chosen by his grandfather in the spring of 1227.

The order of events is unclear, but this is one possible scenario:

The Tangut emperor arrives at Genghis's tent-palace, only to find that the khan 'kept the door closed and made Burkhan pay homage outside the tent'. Moreover, as *The Secret History* relates, Genghis 'felt revulsion within his heart'. This is very odd. Surely the khan, the creator of an empire already twice as large as Rome's, would not willingly deal with his vanquished foe in such a fashion, when by doing so he must have raised suspicions in the minds of Li Xian and his entourage? There is one possible explanation. Genghis and his inner circle had no choice, because Genghis was simply too sick to hold an audience face to face. Of course, the Tangut emperor was going to be killed anyway. But it was important that he make his submission and offer his gifts, completing the ritual that would hand his kingdom to Genghis (or his heir). And it was important that the impression remain in the minds of those whose lives were spared – and in the minds of ordinary Mongols – that Genghis was still in control.

We are told that Genghis survived only a week from the onset of his illness. It would have taken the Xi Xia emperor, with his entourage and laden carts, about that time, perhaps a little longer, to cover the 300 kilometres from his capital to the Mongol HQ. Meanwhile, Genghis was in the Liupan base for treatment. Surely only his imminent death would have brought his treatment to an end. And only in the security of that valley would his grieving entourage be able to follow his instructions to keep his approaching death secret, and then spirit their sick lord out for the showdown in Kaicheng, with Li Xian, puzzled but compliant, laying out his offerings: a set of golden Buddhas followed by other gifts, each one in nines, the number traditionally considered suitable for tribute – golden and silver bowls, boys, girls, geldings, camels and much more, all in nines. Then a senior general saw to the execution, probably by strangulation to observe the ancient tradition which forbade the shedding of noble blood.

No details leaked out, but Genghis apparently had time to give his last order: the Mongols were to exterminate 'the Tangut people's mothers and fathers down to the offspring of their offspring'. Then, he said, 'While I take my meals, you must talk about the killing and destruction of the Tangut, and say "Maimed and tamed, they are no more." ' This, like his previous order, sounds genocidal. Many think it was, given the virtual disappearance of Tangut culture – the language all but lost, the script forgotten, the royal burial-towers stripped of their gorgeous tile cladding to stand stark and grey against the Helan mountains. In fact, the order must have been restricted to the Tangut leaders' families, for – as *The Secret History* relates – 'a great part of the Tangut people was given to Yisui', the wife Genghis had brought with him, the one who ten years before had urged him to choose an heir.

In the history of warfare, Genghis's tactics against both the Muslims of Khorazm and the Tanguts of Xi Xia were brutal in the extreme. But they did not amount to holocaust or genocide, because they were not intended to exterminate a whole race or culture; nor were they early examples of ethnic cleansing. He unleashed no visceral,

GENGHIS'S LEADERSHIP SECRET NO. 20

# PLAN FOR ETERNITY

There was an iron logic behind Genghis's rule. If, as he believed, Heaven had chosen him and his people to rule the world, then it was the empire, not him, that mattered. He was merely the tool through which Heaven's will was becoming manifest. It was up to him as Heaven's tool to ensure that nothing upset progress towards fulfilment of the grand design – world rule, for ever. His death should therefore be no more than a minor setback. The only way to make it so was to keep it a secret, known to only a few essential insiders. Otherwise, every subject nation would revolt, every enemy be heartened, and all would be lost. That is why, I believe, no stories spread about how and where he died, or how his body was treated, or the route his cortège took back to Mongolia. By then, of course, his death was public knowledge. But it didn't matter. The Tanguts were destroyed, the succession was secure, plans for future campaigns were already in hand; Heaven's will had been obeyed.

irrational hatred. Genghis had nothing personal against other tribes or races, as long as they did as they were told. Nor did he indulge in or condone torture or the humiliation of prisoners. His attitudes were businesslike through and through, and might be expressed like this: We Mongols are Heaven's own people, that's the way things are; accept it, get over it, join us, and reap the benefits. So, in dealing with the Tanguts, he saw a problem to be solved. Their leaders had to be punished for their double disloyalty, of course, and their armies taken out, but this was a mere stumbling block on his way to the solution to a far more significant problem: the final conquest of Jin. He was, like a kung-fu fighter, punching straight through Xi Xia, removing it from the field of play, in order instantly to move on and complete the job he had started sixteen years before. Unfortunately, death came knocking on his *ger*-door, and delayed things.

According to some later Chinese sources, Genghis died on the twelfth day of the seventh lunar month: 25 August. But the most reliable Chinese accounts date from a decade later, at best, after the Mongol conquest of Jin was complete, and not all others agree on the exact day. *The Secret History*, which should be the most reliable source, says nothing at all on this subject, except that Genghis 'ascended to Heaven' – proof enough, I think, that the time and place of his death were to remain a state secret.

The secrecy, which was such a vital part of his last act of leadership, ensured that rumour conquered all. Stories multiplied that Genghis died besieging some city or other; or that he survived until the surrender of Xi Xia. And later – decades later, centuries later – poets and storytellers recalled the great man's passing, hiding the few known facts beneath a tangle of anachronistic lore, much of it Buddhist.

His burial remained a part of the secret, as he intended. The funeral cortège that carried his body north-ward across the Gobi would surely have been a simple one – a single cart, accompanied by family, officers and outriders – because, this being summer, speed was of the essence. Later legend spoke of the mass slaughter of anyone who saw the procession, supposedly to preserve the secret; but this dramatic detail was derived from Marco

Polo, and he was speaking of a later emperor, Mönkhe, who had died fourteen years before Marco arrived in China. It seems to me that this would have been disastrous, drawing attention to the cortège and alienating the survivors, flying in the face of Genghis's express wishes and the interests of his people.

A speedy journey, and then what? Surely not the grand burial that so many imagine, on the grounds that other, lesser monarchs had vast wealth to accompany them in the afterlife. There is no burial mound, and almost certainly no lavish grave containing riches drawn from all Eurasia. His wishes had been implied by his 1219 letter to Changchun: 'I live in the wild regions of the north . . . I return to simplicity, I turn again to purity.' So almost certainly he was given a simple burial on or nearby Burkhan Khaldun, the sacred mountain on which his life had been saved as a 20-year-old. Horses were driven over the sacred site to disguise the exact spot, which was then surrounded at a discreet distance by guards. For some years it was a taboo area, until grass and saplings grew and the site was lost to memory. Now the only firm belief is that he lies somewhere on the slopes of this bulky, flat-topped mountain, or in one of its adjacent valleys.

This was as he willed it; and no general, wife, brother or son would have gone against his wishes. To death and beyond, he was the leader.

# 8

# LEGACY: FAILURE, COLLAPSE AND A MEMORY OF GLORY

GENGHIS TREATED his empire – bridging the Pacific and the Caspian, an area four times the size of Alexander's and twice the size of Rome's – like a family estate, dividing it between his surviving three sons and the two sons of his eldest, Jochi, who had died. His heir as Great Khan was, as decreed, his third son Ogedei, who took over the newly conquered territory in north China, the administrative apparatus and his father's vision: the unfinished business of conquest.

It was Ogedei, therefore, who resumed the attack on north China, and completed this part of his father's work in 1234. He inherited a wreck, ruined by war, the migration of refugees and disease: a wreck which might have crumbled further had not Chucai convinced Ogedei that taxation was a more fruitful policy than extermination. Even so, Mongol records – meticulously gathered by the new secretariat – suggest that the population had dropped catastrophically from 40 million to 10 million since the first invasion some 25 years previously.[1]

---

[1] Probably more a reflection of the numbers of cross-border refugees than of deaths.

It was also Ogedei who reopened the assault westward, sending armies across Russia into Poland and Hungary, knocking out cities by the dozen and branding nightmare visions of doom into Russian and European folk memory. European leaders froze like deer in headlights, waiting for slaughter – which never came, because Ogedei's drunken death in 1241 called the armies home, leaving a wilderness of burned towns, decomposing bodies and populations reduced to cannibalism. What might have happened had these brilliant and implacable forces been under Genghis's more subtle command is anyone's guess. They never went back, possibly because their brief stay had revealed that Hungary's pastures were not after all big enough to fuel a horse-borne invasion of western Europe.

It all nearly collapsed. A decade of squabbling seemingly ended when a grandson, Mönkhe, emerged as khan. Another campaign renewed the assault on Islam, knocked out Baghdad and continued westward, eventually shuddering to a halt in a major

*A near collapse, another push westward and a new emperor.*

defeat in southern Israel in 1261. By then Mönkhe was dead, the army reduced in numbers and weakened from lack of grass. Again, it ran out of fuel.

It was another of Genghis's grandsons, Mönkhe's brother Kublai, who now claimed the imperial mantle. By this point the vast estate Genghis had bequeathed was more like four sub-empires, a federation divided by rival ambitions, held together only by residual family loyalties. Kublai, too, clung to his grandfather's dream of infinite conquest. He spent his life in its pursuit, with consequences which affect us all today. For it was this dream that inspired Kublai to create China pretty much as it is now.

In order to fulfil Genghis's vision, Kublai had to take the rest of China – Song, as it was known. This was a ludicrously ambitious proposition. Song was the world's grandest kingdom: 70 million people, over twice the size and with many times the wealth of north China and Mongolia put together. It was the Chinese heartland, the fertile plains watered by the Yangtze and Yellow Rivers, which for millennia had nurtured a culture of unrivalled artistry, wealth and depth of thought, by comparison with which Islam was a mere newcomer, while Europe was still locked into a pre-Renaissance dark age. It had 50,000 kilometres of river highways and merchant ships of unmatched sophistication, trading from ports richer than any others in the world. Annual revenues from maritime customs duty alone amounted to 65 billion coins annually. It printed books by the million, and paper money. It was everything the Mongols were not. Yet this was Kublai's intended prey.

To assault it, Kublai first took the independent kingdom of Nanzhao, which when finally conquered in 1253 became the Chinese province of Yunnan. At the same time, in preparation for the invasion of the south, he built on a pre-existing relationship with Tibet, a relationship established by his cousin Köten in 1246. He did so because he needed an ideology different from and also grander than the local creeds of Mongolia and China: shamanism, Confucianism, Daoism and a smatter of Christianity.[2] He

---

[2] In its Nestorian form. Nestorian missionaries were active all over Central Asia and China. Kublai's mother was a Nestorian, and so was the wife of another of her sons, the emperor Mönkhe.

found it in Tibetan Buddhism, which provided him with the concept of a 'universal emperor' – an ideology that justified world conquest. By adopting this form of Buddhism, he would become head of both church and state in an empire linking Mongol, Chinese, Tibetan, Tangut and any other culture that might come his way by conquest or submission in the future. Like his grandfather, he saw the need for a script to unify this world empire. His Tibetan Buddhist guru, Phags-pa, devised for him a new script, derived from Tibetan sources, which would be used to write all the languages of all his subjects, past, present and future. With Yunnan and Tibet secured, with Mongolia his by definition, with all lands westward, including the regions now known as Xinjiang, owing allegiance, he was in a position to assault the south. This immense 20-year series of campaigns was eventually completed in 1279, a shock almost as catastrophic to the Song elite as the conquest of Islam was to Muslims. Rather than submit, many hundreds committed suicide.

This was the high point of the Mongol empire. For the next fifteen years it was possible for Kublai to claim allegiance from family members ruling from the Pacific to the eastern fringe of Hungary, from the Urals to the Persian Gulf. By any standards, this was an astonishing tribute to the vision of Genghis Khan.

## Genghis's grand vision: insanity revealed

But it was also far too big to hold together. Chinese unity was won at the expense of imperial collapse.

In theory it could have worked. There was a nominal

unity, imposed first by the memory of Genghis, second by his vision of world ownership, and third by a terrific communications system, which the Mongols had in the form of a pony express that could deliver messages across the empire at full gallop. Equipped with relay stations and spare horses and expert riders and special passes, it routinely achieved speeds of several hundred kilometres a day. Kublai bequeathed a network of some 1,400 relay stations, employing over 44,000 horses – 30 per station, on average. In theory, a message could cross the empire in a couple of weeks, though in practice the system was much abused. Still, abused or not, there was nothing like it until the coming of the telegraph. Even trains were slower, because by the time the railways came in the nineteenth century travel was held up by national frontiers.

The problem was that the vision itself was – of course – totally insane. Genghis himself would have seen that, if he had known the true size and variety of Eurasia, let alone the world. His own world consisted of Mongolia and its neighbouring peoples: big enough, to be sure, but a mere fraction of the whole. Nor did he understand at first that Mongol expansion was fuelled by grass, and where the grass ran out his writ could no longer run. Any extension beyond the grasslands – as he discovered, with a flexibility that amounted to genius – demanded new technology, new peoples, new forms of warfare, constant adaptation.

Well, he was almost up to the task in his lifetime, and his conquests had a momentum that carried beyond his death. But then, when his heirs reached beyond the limits, the history of the empire became one of stuttering progress, followed by dissipation and collapse, drawn out over 150 years. It was not simply that the later Mongol rulers came up against ecological and administrative limits. They came up against each other, against the limits of human nature. Kublai's relatives ruling in today's Central Asia, Iraq, Iran, Saudi Arabia and southern Russia acquired their own ambitions, responded to their local needs, turned Islamic, became jealous of each other's reach, made alliances with foreign powers against each other, fought each other, taxed their subjects to death, and remained despised by them until they were slung from power.

In what should have remained the heartland of empire, Kublai himself exemplified the problems. To rule here he needed to span two worlds, Mongol and Chinese, preserving the Mongol elite while ruling his Chinese subjects. He could not rule China from the Mongol capital of Karakorum: it was too far from China, too Mongol. So he made himself two capitals south of the Gobi. One was on the grasslands, his Upper Capital, Shang Du (which English speakers know as Xanadu), where he spent his summers playing at being a Mongol, with tents and hunting grounds described by Marco Polo. The other was his rebuilt Beijing.[3] Much of his time he spent commuting between the two, the outward and visible symbol of a precarious balancing act that could not work, because it separated him from the traditional horse-breeding grounds of the steppes on which Mongol power had always rested.

At the same time as overseeing a vast administrative machine – no mean feat of management – Kublai remained

---

[3] Beijing is today's name. The city has had many. When Genghis took it in 1215 it was Zhongdu (Central Capital). Under Kublai, it became Dadu (Great Capital), but was popularly known as Khan-balikh, the Khan's City.

obsessed by his grandfather's vision. China was to be the engine for further expansion. His prime target was Japan; in pursuit of it, two invasion fleets were lost to storms, the first in 1274, the second, notoriously, in 1281, after the unification of China under Mongol rule had opened up new possibilities: huge ports, shipbuilding capacity, crews and soldiers by the million. His fleet numbered some 4,400 ships. With a few hundred massive battleships and the rest the equivalent of landing craft, this was the largest naval force in world history to date, and remained so until the Allied invasion of Europe in 1944. It also symbolized everything that was wrong with Kublai's leadership. Orders came from the top by diktat and were passed on by corrupt officials to surly workforces in Korean and Chinese ports; ships were cobbled together with no quality control and manned by unwilling crews. An unshared vision, shoddy workmanship, deceptive subordinates eager only to escape censure: it was a catastrophe waiting to happen. Even with good weather and superb organization, it probably wouldn't have worked. And, as better reconnaissance would have shown, the Japanese were ready for them. They had used the previous seven years to unify their command structures and build a wall that would have been enough to keep the Mongol, Chinese and Korean forces on the beaches. In the event, they did not need to fight. By the time Kublai's delayed and unready fleets met up off the Japanese coast, the typhoon season was upon them. In mid-August, the sea off present-day Fukuoka became a giant blender, swirling Kublai's fleet into a soup of wooden splinters, burying it in mud, and drowning some 65,000: almost certainly the greatest seaborne catastrophe in history. Only now are bits of the fleet emerging from the

GENGHIS'S LEADERSHIP SECRET NO. 21

## KNOW YOUR LIMITS

From beyond the grave, Genghis would have had sound advice for his grandson, Kublai. 'Remember leadership secret no. 9: Get real. With the wisdom of hindsight, I see I misunderstood Heaven's will. My world was not the whole world. You have found your limits. Respect them! See what happens if you don't: you forget your roots, you pretend to be Chinese, you are forced into displays of wealth, you are corrupted by luxury, your people are not your people, and you cannot be generous to them all. I made myself loved, because I was strong enough to afford generosity. Though your heart is good, you will make yourself hated because you have attempted the impossible and weakened yourself. Listen to me before it is too late: withdraw northward, where the skies are blue and life is pure. Forget China, or she will have her revenge upon us.' But Kublai was bound by a vision that had become an ideology. He had lost the flexibility that had underpinned his grandfather's genius. By attempting the impossible, he set his new dynasty on the long, slow road to ruin.

slurry in a research programme headed by marine archaeologist Kenzo Hayashida, whose museum on Takashima Island displays the evidence of the fleet's unreadiness.[2]

Still Kublai would not awake from this dream – this nightmare – of conquest. He even wanted to mount a third invasion of Japan, until disasters elsewhere forced him to

[2] For a detailed account of the disaster and the archaeological research into it, see my *Kublai Khan*, ch. 13.

abandon the idea. There were campaigns to seize Burma (twice, in 1277 and 1284), Vietnam (1286–8) and Java (1292): all failures. At home, the cost of these adventures was catastrophic. Not only was the economy over-stretched, but Kublai relied on a corrupt Uzbek finance minister named Ahmad to wring wealth from his unhappy subjects. In the end, in 1282, just after the Japan disaster, plotters devised a lunatic scheme involving a mock-prince and rent-a-crowd followers who inveigled Ahmad out of Beijing and murdered him. Nothing could have better revealed how out of touch Kublai was – now in his late sixties, depressed at the death of his favourite wife, vastly overweight and an alcoholic. The three western sub-empires ruled by his feuding relatives had long since gone their own ways, while a slab of Central Asia had for years been claimed, with greater and lesser degrees of success, by a rebellious cousin, Kaidu. Kublai died aged 79 at the end of January 1294, and was buried near his grandfather on the holy mountain of the Mongols, Burkhan Khaldun.

Why did it go wrong? Well, in some ways it didn't, because to hold such a mammoth, impossible edifice together at all was an extraordinary achievement. But the plain fact is that it collapsed, for three fundamental reasons:

- Kublai's vision of world rule was not only unattainable, it was inauthentic: not his own, but his grandfather's. If he had been as talented a leader as Genghis he would have been able to modify it to suit new realities – the rivalries of his relatives, the surliness of his Han subjects, the size and complexity of the world – without sinking into the lunacy of attempting to exceed his grasp with campaigns that sucked up money like black holes.

- His leadership itself was inauthentic, for he was an outsider. His people were not his people; only his staff were – the officers, the administrators, the secret service. His rule was the top-down variety, which like all despotisms, is vulnerable to corrosion from the bottom up.

- Like his grandfather, he had no message for humankind. Not that the Yuan Dynasty lacked for great artists and writers – Yuan ceramics, Yuan theatre, Yuan painting, Yuan craftsmanship all still evoke intense admiration. But they were Chinese creations, not Mongol, sometimes achieved with the support of Kublai's court, sometimes despite him. But he himself had nothing significant to say.

Ultimately, Kublai's rule underlined a truth about the relationship between power and leadership: they are not necessarily the same. Kublai was the most powerful man of his era, perhaps the most powerful ruler in world history until the emergence of modern superpowers. He was a great manager, a mediocre strategist, and he did his best; but that is not the same as being a great leader.

After Kublai's death there was nothing much left of the empire but tenuous links back to Genghis. In Persia, Mongol rule vanished 30 years later. In southern Russia, former Mongols turned Islamic, communicating in Turkish. In Central Asia, the third Mongol sub-empire fell to Tamerlane, who claimed to be a reincarnation of Genghis, though he was not in a direct line of descent.

Still, the name echoed down the centuries after his descendants seized much of India as the Mughals. In China, Kublai's heirs struggled with his legacy for another 73 years, while power seeped away in a sequence of disputed successions, conspiracies, assassinations and civil strife, not to mention plague and inflation. In 1368 rebellion drove 60,000 of the top Mongols back to the grasslands, leaving several hundred thousand to be taken over by the incoming Ming, who ruled China until themselves displaced by the Manchus in 1644.

## Genghis's enduring vision

That, you might think, was pretty much that for Genghis's crazy dream of world rule. Not quite. The nation he created remains intact, and his image there re-emerged after 70 years of Communist rule as bright as ever. So keen are the Mongols to name every conceivable consumer product after him that the government is considering legislation to outlaw the practice, or rather to allow his name to be used only by official permission, which will no doubt cost quite a few tugriks.

The fact that the dream faltered is not surprising; it was a dream impossible to realize as a whole. But it has survived in part, in the shape and extent of today's China. For it was in pursuit of that dream that Kublai annexed Yunnan and Tibet, and claimed authority over the western provinces of Gansu, Ningxia and Xinjiang, doing his best to dispute them with his cousin Kaidu. And it is in consequence of his failures that China does not now include Burma, Vietnam, Java or Japan.

This was the China inherited by the Ming when the

Mongols were overthrown in 1368. As the Japanese scholar Hidehiro Okada states, the only possible justification for the Ming claim to sovereignty over these non-Han areas 'was the claim that the Ming emperors were legitimate successors to the Mongol khans'. It was the same with the Manchus when they took over in 1644. And again with modern China, which claims Tibet and the unruly Muslim lands of Xinjiang because Kublai, a Mongol, had claimed them in the name of his grandfather.

By several quirks of fate, Mongolia itself slipped away from the Chinese family and fell into the arms of the new Soviet Union in 1921. Unfortunately for traditionalists in China, Mongolia's independence was confirmed by plebiscite in 1945, the result being recognized by China four years before the Communist victory, thus forestalling any attempt by Mao to regain control, as he did in Tibet in 1950.

Mongolia endures, thanks in large part to Genghis's genius. The same goes for China. It is one of history's great ironies that China should owe its geographical reach – its territorial identity – to the ambitions and convictions of a 20-year-old fugitive in a remote part of twelfth-century Mongolia. Together, these two nations reflect Genghis's original dream, a dream so overblown it is astonishing that any of it was realized. Together, they comprise a quarter of humanity and one-twelfth of the world's land area. These bare facts alone are evidence of a vision and a quality of leadership that have no rivals.

# APPENDIX:
# GETTING THE MEASURE OF GENGHIS'S GENIUS

WITH THE HELP of modern leadership theory, it is possible to anatomize many of the qualities that made Genghis exceptional. Daniel Goleman, who popularized the notion of emotional intelligence (EI), is my guide, if only because one of Genghis's overriding characteristics was the way he could react emotionally, understand his own emotions, and allow them to infuse his decisions, without being controlled by them.

Clearly, this exercise does not offer a complete explanation. A theory devised to assess leadership in democracies and market economies today cannot apply 100 per cent to clan-based, military leadership 800 years ago. But Goleman's parameters and Genghis's leadership skills are both wide enough for there to be a considerable overlap.

Take the matter of emotional self-control:

Genghis has often been compared with Hitler, because of their towering ambitions, ruthlessness and destructiveness. But look more closely: compare Genghis's many positive qualities with Hitler's negativity, in particular his self-control with Hitler's notorious irrationality. On one occasion the Führer became enraged to the point of temporary insanity, 'hurling himself to the floor and chewing the edge of the carpet' – an outburst that inspired the nickname *Teppichfresser*, 'Carpet-eater'.[1] Such behaviour is totally alien to Genghis's personality. Nor would Genghis have allowed himself to be driven by wishful thinking into underestimating an opponent, as Hitler was after the Japanese assault on Pearl Harbor in December 1941, when he called the United States a 'decayed country' that would soon collapse; he then declared war on America, without provocation or need, just for the prestige of striking the first blow, thus condemning Germany to defeat. This was government by personality, not for reasons of state. With Genghis, the cause came first, emotions second.

To compare his qualities with the 'leadership competencies' identified by Goleman and his associates is not comparing like with like. Modern leaders do not have the freedoms to dream up grand visions on the scale of Genghis's, let alone execute them (though in terms of ambition alone Mao got close in the late 1950s, with his plan for world domination. Not that this went far in practical terms, given that he was prepared to sacrifice millions of his own people.)

Nor are Goleman's categories absolute. They overlap; some of them do not apply to Genghis; and Genghis had traits that do not apply in the modern world (his extreme vision and his extreme ruthlessness, to name two).

Goleman's eighteen 'competencies' break down into two groups and four sub-groups:

---

[1] Shirer, *The Rise and Fall of the Third Reich*, p. 478.

personal competence:
- self-awareness (3);
- self-management (6);

social competence:
- social awareness (3);
- relationship management (6).

# Personal competence

SELF-AWARENESS

## 1 Emotional self-awareness

*Reading one's own emotions and understanding how they affect one's decision-making and one's colleagues.*

Genghis was no psychopath, no lover of violence for its own sake. He was a man of powerful and very human emotions. As the story of Bekhter's murder shows, he was well aware of the dangers of unrestrained emotion. He loved his sons, his four adopted sons and his grandsons. His rather active sex life was that of an alpha male, taking pleasure, to be sure, but also asserting status. Yet he held several women in high respect: his mother, of course, and at least three of his wives: Börte, his senior wife, the Tatar Yisui, who was captured when her tribe was crushed and became a powerful influence later, and her younger sister, who was captured first.

An aside on this younger one, Yisügen. She must have been a beauty, but she also made astute use of her charm to demand respect and also help her sister. 'Being loved by him, [she] said, "If it pleases the khan, he will take care of me, regarding me as a human being and person worth keeping. But my elder sister, who is called Yisui, is superior to me: she is more suitable for a ruler."' Genghis was interested, and ordered a search for Yisui. 'But,' he added, 'if your elder sister comes to hand, will you yield your place to her?' Yes, she would; and yes, she did. That was how Yisui was 'placed in the rank of his principal wives'. Note the genuine emotion, and the consideration.

## 2  Accurate self-assessment

*Knowing one's strengths and weaknesses, combined with a willingness to accept criticism.*
When he rewarded two of his closest friends, he praised them because:

> *You urged me to carry out what was right,*
> *You persuaded me not to do what was wrong.*

Flexibility, a readiness to change heart: these are not qualities you associate with a man noted for his ruthlessness and brutality.

## 3  Self-confidence

No comment. When you know the world is yours by Heaven's command, you do not lack for self-confidence.

SELF-MANAGEMENT
## 4  Emotional self-control

*The ability to keep disruptive emotions under control.*
Nothing came between Genghis and his cause. Despite the image of two young lovers embracing in the moonlight when he rescued Börte from the Merkits, he was not a man to forget himself. After all, it was his decision to save himself rather than fight for Börte that led to her capture in the first place. He accepted Jochi as his son, despite the doubt over his paternity; yet when Jochi disobeyed him –

Jochi had argued with his brothers and Genghis ordered him back to sort out the dispute – Genghis was prepared to crush him, and might even have ordered his assassination. Even when using extreme violence, he knew very well what he was doing, and was just as able to exercise restraint as to order mass executions. There was no emotional self-indulgence. He learned that early, when he allowed his emotions to rule him and killed his half-brother Begter, and ever after remembered his mother's reprimand.

## 5  Transparency
*Displaying honesty and integrity.*
As he learned from Jamukha as a young blood, a leader's word is his bond. *The Secret History*, always concerned to reflect Genghis's views, is careful to show that he never broke his word again. Jamukha and Toghril betrayed Genghis, but he never responded in kind. Mistakes (at least those mistakes from which his people could learn lessons) were admitted.

## 6  Adaptability
*Flexibility in adapting to changing situations.*
Genghis owed much of his empire and its effective administration to a readiness to adapt. The concept of national unity was not new, but the policy of forcing it through with ruthlessness was something that sprang from Genghis's emotional drives and his imagination. He could not have foreseen where all this might lead, yet once he saw the new needs his policy had created, he responded. The adoption of writing, the establishment of a bureaucracy and the creation of records were all adaptations to new demands.

## 7   Achievement
*The drive to improve performance to meet inner standards of excellence.*
No doubt about this one: writing, laws, social revolution and upgrading his army were all examples of improvements in his own leadership and in his organization. As Goleman and his colleagues write, 'A hallmark of achievement is in continual learning – and teaching – ways to do better.'

## 8   Initiative
*Readiness to act and seize opportunities.*
As a strategist and tactician, Genghis was superb at creating and seizing opportunities. A small example: the way he saw the potential in the sable coat that was given to his mother, and his use of it to solicit Toghril's support. A large one: his risky decision to invade Khorazm.

## 9   Optimism
*An ability to retain one's vision and sustain hope.*
He had the capacity to inspire in his followers the feeling that, despite setbacks, tomorrow will be better than today. With Genghis, optimism is an implied trait of his leadership, because his vision was so grand and his successes so manifest that tomorrow was *always* going to be better.

# Social competence

SOCIAL AWARENESS
## 10   Empathy
*An ability to attune to a wide range of emotional signals.*
Despite his insistence that his people were the best, he

could get along well with almost anyone, if need be. Genghis's empathy was manifest in both his curiosity and his determination to make his empire work by employing people of diverse backgrounds, former enemies or not: Naiman, Merkit, Tatar, Khitan, Muslim, Uighur, Chinese.

## 11 Organizational awareness

*Political astuteness; an ability to detect significant social networks and power relationships.*

This was a crucial ability, especially in the early days, when one wrong move in the shifting world of steppe politics could have been disastrous. In particular, he needed to be able to balance the needs for self-preservation and independence with the benefits and dangers of making or breaking alliances.

## 12 Service

*An ability to foster an emotional climate in which he served his subordinates while they served him.*

Genghis was at pains to keep his 'clients' – i.e. his people – content by making sure that his own spirit of generosity filtered down, so that commitment from below remained strong. Khanship involved a two-way relationship: the khan delivered vision, strategic direction and booty, while his people responded with self-sacrificial obedience and loyalty.

RELATIONSHIP MANAGEMENT

## 13 Inspiration

*Creating 'resonance with a vision or shared mission so compelling that others willingly follow'.*

Goleman places this way down his list, but it should really

be at the top. Genghis offered the grandest of all visions: world conquest at Heaven's command. Every conquest reinforced the idea. As far as his horses ranged – from the Pacific to southern Russia – it seemed that every nation was destined to fall in line and accept Mongol rule. On his death, no one doubted that all China was a legitimate target, and would eventually succumb. With no awareness of what forces might set limits, there was for a time no reason to doubt that the whole world would eventually acknowledge Mongol overlordship.

## 14   Influence
*The ability to persuade individuals and groups.*
This talent comes into its own when the power to compel is lacking. Once established, Genghis had little need to be persuasive. But on the way up he showed particular skill in acquiring his trusted companions, and in approaching the Kereyid khan Toghril, appealing to his moral sense as his father's 'sworn friend', smoothing the way by offering his mother's sable coat.

## 15   Developing others
*Showing a genuine interest in cultivating people's abilities.*
Poor leaders often see the talents displayed by others as a threat. Genghis encouraged, ignoring both background and racial origins. His adopted brother or son, the Tatar Shigi, became his head of chancery, despite being the child of an enemy tribe. Muqali was left entirely alone as viceroy of half-conquered Jin. Genghis might have said, as I heard a successful and generous-minded CEO say once, 'I have been lucky enough to employ people who are smarter than me.'

## 16   Change catalyst
*Recognizing the need for change, and championing the new order.*
Genghis certainly did that, since he reformed his whole society, and set it on the path to empire.

## 17   Conflict management
*The ability to release and control different viewpoints.*
Leaders who manage conflict best are able to draw out all parties, understand different perspectives, and then find common ground that all can endorse. This is a talent apparently implied by Genghis's openess to advice from his top aides, who sometimes disagreed. But the sheer power of his authority meant that he rarely needed to manage conflict. He decided, overriding squabbles. Only occasionally did he allow conflict, when it threatened to become toxic if suppressed – for example, in the dispute over his succession.

## 18   Teamwork and collaboration
*The ability to generate collegiality.*
A leader who worked at generating helpfulness and co-operation? Hardly. This was not Genghis's style at all. His inspirational leadership made his men loyal to him, to their new nation and to their ever-growing empire – that was his genius – but the team who could offer advice or criticism remained a tiny one of favoured generals and family. His rule did not foreshadow democracy.

Using these standards, where does Genghis stand as a leader? According to Goleman et al.,

No leader we have ever encountered, no matter how outstanding, has strengths across the board in every one of the EI competencies. Highly effective leaders typically exhibit a critical mass of strength in a half dozen or so EI competencies. Moreover there is no fixed formula for great leadership. There are many paths to excellence, and superb leaders can possess very different personal styles. Still, we find that effective leaders typically demonstrate strengths in at least one competence from each of the four fundamental areas of emotional intelligence.

So: effective leaders tick four boxes; highly effective ones tick six or more. Genghis, over the full course of his life, ticks fifteen out of eighteen, with a question mark over a sixteenth (No. 17, 'Conflict management'). There is more to his leadership than these modern criteria suggest, but in Goleman's terms he ranks as a genius.

# BIBLIOGRAPHY

The basic source for Genghis's life is *The Secret History*, in de Rachewiltz's monumental edition. The standard biography of him is Ratchnevsky's, which also has the best bibliography. On the subject of leadership, two studies were particularly helpful. *Primal Leadership*, by Daniel Goleman, Richard Boyatzis and Annie McKee, applies Goleman's ideas on emotional intelligence to leaders. It discusses a number of traits that fit Genghis's character well. Jim Collins's *Good to Great* analyses the talents of leaders of supremely successful companies. Collins does not address other types of leadership, but his hierarchy of leadership skills matches with great accuracy Genghis's maturing qualities. Genghis was also a brilliant military commander. To set his achievements in context, I mainly drew on the classic Chinese military theoretician Sun Tzu (Sun Zi) and the British military historian John Keegan. My main sources are given in the list that follows.

Bretschneider, E., *Mediaeval Researches from Eastern Asiatic Sources*, 2 vols (London: Kegan Paul, 1888), esp. vol. 1, ch. 3: 'Si Yu Ki', the translation of Li Zhichang's *Journey to the West* (Changchun's journey)

Burns, James MacGregor, *Leadership* (New York and London: Harper & Row, 1978)

Collins, Jim, *Good to Great* (London: Random House, 2001;

publ. in USA by Collins Business)

Coutu, Diane L., 'Putting Leaders on the Couch: A Conversation with Manfred F. R. Kets de Vries', *Harvard Business Review*, January 2004; repr. in *On the Mind of the Leader* (Cambridge, Mass.: Harvard Business School, 2005)

Denning, Stephen, *The Secret Language of Leadership: How Leaders Inspire Action Through Narrative* (San Francisco: Jossey-Bass/Wiley, 2007)

Dixon, Norman, *On the Psychology of Military Incompetence* (London: Random House, 1976; new edn 1994)

Gibbon, Edward, *Decline and Fall of the Roman Empire*, vol. 3 (London: Dent, 1910)

Goleman, Daniel, Richard Boyatzis and Annie McKee, *The New Leaders: Transforming the Art of Leadership into the Science of Results* (London: Time Warner, 2002; publ in USA as *Primal Leadership*, Harvard Business School Press, 2002)

Greene, Robert, *The 33 Strategies of War* (New York: Viking Penguin; London: Profile, 2006)

*Harvard Business Review, On the Mind of the Leader* (Cambridge, Mass.: Harvard Business School, 2005)

Hooper, Alan, and John Potter, *Intelligent Leadership: Creating a Passion for Change* (London: Random House, 2001)

Hurd, Russell, 'A Teenager Revisits her Father's Death during Childhood: A Study in Resilience and Healthy Mourning', *Adolescence* (San Diego), vol. 39, no. 154

Janis, I. L., *Victims of Groupthink* (Boston: Houghton Mifflin, 1972)

Juvaini, Ata-Malik, *Genghis Khan: The History of the World-Conqueror*, trans. and ed. J. A. Boyle (Manchester: Manchester University Press, 1958; new edn 1997)

Keegan, John, *A History of Warfare* (London: Random House, 1994)

Keegan, John, *The Mask of Command* (London: Jonathan Cape, 1987)

Kellerman, Barbara, *Bad Leadership: What It Is, How It Happens, Why It Matters* (Cambridge, Mass.: Harvard Business School Press, 2004)

Krueger, John R., *Poetical Passages in the Erdeni-yin Tobči,* (The Hague: Mouton, 1961)

Leighton, Allan, *On Leadership: Practical Wisdom from the People Who Know* (London: Random House, 2007)

Li Zhichang, *Journey to the West* (*Xīyóujì* / 西游): see Bretschneider; Waley

Man, John, *Genghis Khan: Life, Death and Resurrection* (London: Transworld, 2004)

Man, John, *Kublai Khan: The Mongol King Who Remade China* (London: Transworld, 2007)

Martin, H. Desmond, *The Rise of Chingis Khan and his Conquest of North China* (New York: Octagon, 1971)

Meng-Ta Pei-Lu [Mengda Beilu] and Hei-Ta Shih-Lüeh [Heida Shilue], *Chinesische Gesandtenberichte über die Frühen Mongolen 1221 und 1237,* trans. Peter Olbricht and Elisabeth Pinks (Wiesbaden: Harrassowitz, 1980)

Mote, F. W., *Imperial China 900–1800* (Cambridge, Mass. and London: Harvard University Press, 1999)

Nye, Joseph S., *The Powers to Lead* (Oxford: Oxford University Press, 2008)

Okada, Hidehiro, 'China as a Successor State to the Mongol Empire', in Reuven Amitai-Preiss and David Morgan (eds), *The Mongol Empire and its Legacy* (Leiden and Boston: Brill, 1999)

Peter, Laurence J., and Raymond Hull, *The Peter Principle: Why Things Always Go Wrong* (New York: William Morrow, 1968)

Rachewiltz, Igor de, 'Yeh-lü Ch'u-ts'ai, Yeh-lü Chu, Yeh-lü

Hsi-liang', in Igor de Rachewiltz et al. (eds), *In the Service of the Khan: Eminent Personalities of the Early Mongol–Yüan Era (1200–1300)* (Wiesbaden: Harrassowitz, 1973)

Rachewiltz, Igor de (trans. and commentary), *The Secret History of the Mongols: A Mongolian Epic Chronicle of the 13th Century*, 2 vols (Leiden and Boston: Brill, 2004)

Rachewiltz, Igor de, 'The Title Čingis Qan / Qaγan Re-Examined' in Walter Heissig and Klaus Sagaster (eds), *Gedanke und Wirkung: Festschrift zum 90. Geburtstag von Nikolaus Poppe* (Wiesbaden: Harrassowitz, 1989)

Ratchnevsky, Paul, *Genghis Khan: His Life and Legacy*, trans. and ed. Thomas Haining (Oxford: Blackwell, 1991)

Rossabi, Morris, *Khubilai Khan: His Life and Times* (Berkeley, Los Angeles and London: University of California Press, 1983)

Shirer, William, *The Rise and Fall of the Third Reich* (London: Secker & Warburg, 1960)

Siebert, Al, *The Survivor Personality* (Portland, Oreg.: Practical Psychology Press, 1993)

Slim, Gen. Sir William, *Defeat into Victory* (London: Cassell, 1956)

Sun Tzu (Sun Zi), *The Art of War*, with Shang Yang, *The Book of Lord Shang* (Ware: Wordsworth, 1998)

Waley, Arthur (trans.), *The Travels of an Alchemist: The Journey of the Taoist Ch'ang-Chun from China to the Hindukush at the Summons of Chingiz Khan, Recorded by his Disciple Li Chih-chang* (London: Routledge, 1934)

Weber, Maximilian, *Theory of Social and Economic Organization*, trans. A. R. Anderson and Talcott Parsons (New York: Free Press, 1964)

Worden, J. William, *Children and Grief: When a Parent Dies* (New York and London: Guilford Press, 1996)

# INDEX

Afghanistan 82, 122, 130, 131
Ahmad (finance minister)
    157–8
Alexander the Great 56, 78, 79,
    110, 111, 122, 133
Ambakai 31, 41, 81
Amin, Idi 63
*anda* oath 28–30, 67
Aristotle 125
Asano, Tadanobu 4
Asha (Tangut general) 110,
    138–9
Attila the Hun 62–4

Baghdad 99, 118, 151
Baljuna Covenant 54–5, 57
Begter (Genghis's half-brother)
    31–2, 33, 166
Beijing 51, 90, 91, 92–4, 106,
    110, 155
Bennis, Warren 38
Bodrov, Sergei: *Mongol* 4–5, 82n
Boorchu 37
Börte (Genghis's wife) 37, 39,
    43, 46, 47, 75, 103, 164, 165

Branson, Richard 28
Buddhism 65, 127, 132, 135,
    146, 148
    Tibetan 153
Bukhara 99, 100, 113, 116–17
Burkhan Khaldun 13, 17, 18,
    39, 49, 149, 158
Burma 12, 158, 160
Burns, James MacGregor:
    *Leadership* 7, 56

Carlyle, Thomas 2
Chagadai (Genghis's son) 104,
    113, 115
Changchun 127, 128–32, 134,
    149
Charlemagne, Holy Roman
    Emperor 40
China/Chinese
    attitude to Mongols 21, 23
    communications system 154
    Daoism 132
    division into empires 80–1
    and Kublai Khan 3, 151–6
    Manchu dynasty 160, 161

China/Chinese (*cont.*)
  Mandate of Heaven 40, 41,
    53, 66, 106
  Ming dynasty 160
  Mongol legal system 71, 72
  Ogedei's conquest 150
  writers on war 86, 108–9, 126
  Yuan dynasty 3, 159
  *see also* Jin dynasty; Song
    dynasty; Xi Xia empire
Christianity 19, 40, 135
  Nestorian 42, 43, 126, 154
    *and n*
Chucai *see* Yelü Chucai
Churchill, Winston 21, 55–6
Clinton, Bill 28
Collins, Jim *Good to Great* 57,
  59, 64, 133, 135
Confucius (Kong
  Fuzi)/Confucianism 127, 152
Crimean War (1857) 78, 82

Daoism 125, 127, 128, 131, 132,
  135, 152
Datong 90
Dixon, Norman: *On the
  Psychology of Military
  Incompetence* 77–8, 82

al-Farabi 125
First Emperor, the 8, 127, 142
Freud, Sigmund 28

Genghis Khan (Chingis Khan)
  2–4, 5–6
**biographical details:**
  birth and childhood 23–7, 31
  brothers and half-brothers

    31–2, 37, 74–6
  on Burkhan Khaldun (1181)
    1, 13, 17–18, 39–40
  death 148
  and death of father 25–7
  escape from captivity 34–6
  funeral and tomb 4, 16, 148–9
  and Hoelun, his mother 27–8,
    32, 33, 74–5, 164, 166
  illness and deathbed
    conspiracy 141–8
  injuries 52, 79, 90, 138
  and Jamukha 28–9, 43–5,
    46–9, 58–60
  marriage and wives 37, 39,
    43, 46, 164–5
  names and titles 1, 4*n*, 65–6,
    73
  and naming of his successor
    102–5
**character and personality
  traits** 17
  accurate self-assessment 165
  emotional self-awareness
    164–5
  emotional self-control 162,
    163
  humility 129, 133, 135
  intellectual curiosity 125
  religious and philosophical
    interests 123–7, 128, 130,
    131–3, 133, 136–7
  self-confidence 165
  tolerance 135
  *see also* leadership qualities
    *and* military leadership
    (*below*)
**leadership qualities** vii–viii,

6–7, 8, 12, 41, 163–4
ability to make alliances 36,
  168
acknowledgement of
  inadequacies and
  limitations 61, 62, 63, 157
adaptability to change 166,
  170
belief in divine support
  13–14, 15, 17, 18–21, 40, 73,
  75–6, 79, 123, 147
brutality and use of violence
  49–50, 75–6, 120–1, 146–7
care about detail 69
charisma 11, 14, 132
and core values 53, 69
cultivation of people's
  abilities 169
cunning 76
drive to improve performance
  167
empathy 32, 167–8
employment of the best 66–8,
  69, 107; see also Yelü
  Chucai
honesty and integrity 166
initiative 167
inspiration 168–9, 170
law making 70–3
making himself symbol of the
  state and its laws 95
military see military
  leadership (below)
openness to advice and
  criticism 33, 45, 105, 165
organizational awareness 168
persuasion and influence 169
recognition of need for

written administration 60–2
religious and philosophical
  interest 125
rewarding of loyalty 52–3,
  66–8, 69, 95
two-way relationship with
  subordinates 168
vision 42, 70, 153, 154, 160–1,
  163, 167, 168–9
**military leadership** 79–80, 88
and Baljuna Covenant 54–5
choice of commanders 66–8,
  112–13, 118
conquests see Jin; Khorazm;
  Tatars; Xi Xia
and importance of military
  intelligence 81–3, 100
introduction of centralized
  control 68–9
ruthlessness 112, 120–1,
  140–1, 146–7, 162, 163
sharing of hardship 54–7,
  69–70
strategies 80, 83–4, 92, 96, 98,
  108–9, 112–13, 114, 139–40,
  142–3
see also Mongol army
Georgia 118
Geronimo 2
Gibbon, Edward: Decline and
  Fall of the Roman Empire
  85–7
Gobi desert 88, 90, 115
Goleman, Daniel, et al.: The
  New Leaders . . . 9, 45, 53,
  70, 162, 163–4, 167, 168,
  170–1
Great Raid, the 118–19

Great Wall of China, the 23, 83
Great Yasa (legal code) 70–1,
72
Gurganj (Urgench), Khorazm
119
Güyük Khan 20, 123

Hada 95–6
Hayashida, Kenzo 157
Helan mountains 88, 89, 138,
146
Henry VIII, King 73
Herat 119
Hitler, Adolf 21, 162–3
Hoelun (Genghis's mother) 25,
27–8, 32, 33, 37, 39, 47,
74–5, 164, 166
Hungary 137, 151, 153
Huns 23, 63–4, 75–7
hunts, Mongolian 84–5, 86

Inalchuk, governor of Otrar
100–1, 115
India 160
Innocent IV, Pope 20, 123
Iran 155
Iraq 50, 82, 114, 155
Islam 41, 135, 151, 153
see also Muslims

Jalal ad-Din 122
James I, King 40
Jamukha 28–9, 37, 43, 44, 45,
46–7, 48, 49–50, 51, 58–9,
166
Janis, I. L.: Victims of
Groupthink 82
Japan 12, 155–7, 160

attack on Pearl Harbor 82,
163
kamikaze pilots 57
Java 12, 158, 160
Jebe 67, 99, 110, 112, 113,
118–19
Jelme 67
Jesus Christ 19, 56
Jin dynasty 21, 61, 80, 106
and Ambakai's death 31, 81
army 89, 90–1
claims Mandate of Heaven 40
Genghis's alliance with 50–1
Genghis's campaigns against
77, 81–3, 90–7, 138, 140,
141, 142–3, 147, 148, 150
and Tanguts (Xi Xia) 83–4,
88–9
Jochi (Genghis's brother) see
Khasar
Jochi (Genghis's son) 46, 104,
113, 115, 150, 165–6
Jurchen, the 51, 80, 81, 83, 98
Juvaini, Ata-Malik: Genghis
Khan . . . 70, 71, 84, 85, 87,
100, 101, 116, 119

Kabul, ruler of the Mongols
(Genghis's great-
grandfather) 21, 23, 31, 41
Kaicheng 144–6
Kaidu 158, 160
Kaifeng 92, 93, 94, 142–3
Kara Khitai 98, 99, 113
Karakorum 155
Keegan, John: The Mask of
Command 22–3, 69, 79
Kellerman, Barbara: Bad

*Leadership* . . . 8, 9
Kereyids, the 37, 38
Kets de Vries, Manfred 23–4, 28
Khara-Khoto 139
Khasar (Jochi; Genghis's brother) 31, 54, 74–5
Khitans 54, 83, 98, 106–7, 168
Khorazm 99
    conquered by Genghis 82, 109–18, 119–22, 138, 167
    *see also* Mohammed, shah of Khorazm
Khorchi 48
Kiriltuk, Taychiut chief 52–3
Kököchu Teb Tengeri 73–4, 75
Kong Fuzi *see* Confucius
Korean forces 156
Köten 152
Krueger, John 15–16
Kublai Khan 1–2, 3, 12, 94, 144–5, 151–9, 160, 161
Kuchlug, prince of the Naimans 98–9, 110
Kyzylkum desert 113, 115

Lattimore, Owen 6
leadership vii, 7–11, 170–1
    acceptance of criticism 32–4, 44, 45, 165
    acknowledgement of inadequacies and limitations 61, 63, 157
    adaptability and flexibility 166, 170
    and character traits 20, 21
    and charisma 10–11, 133–4
    and choice of subordinates vii, 67, 69, 107, 112–13
    and conflict management 170
    core values 53, 69, 70
    and cultivation of others' abilities 169
    and drive to improve performance 167
    and emotional appeal 10
    and emotional intelligence (EI) 162, 170
    and empathy 167–8
    greatness in 11–12
    and humility 135
    importance of presentation 19
    and initiative 167
    integrity and keeping of promises 44–5
    and luck 59
    and management 7
    morale boosting 56–8
    and morality 9, 12, 76
    organizational awareness 168
    and persuasion 7, 9, 169
    the Peter Principle viii *and n*
    and power 7, 8–9, 11, 159
    recognizing importance of role of leader 53
    and 'resonance' 45, 53, 168–9
    right man for right time 21, 22
    rule-making 72
    sharing of hardship and suffering 54–6, 57
    taking responsibility for failure 59
    teamwork and collaboration 170
    top-down 158–9
    and tyranny 7

leadership (*cont.*)
  and vision vii, 11, 42, 69–70,
    167
  *see also* Genghis Khan,
    leadership qualities
legal system, Mongolian 70–3
Legalism 127
Leighton, Allan: *On Leadership*
  107
Li Dewang, Tangut emperor
  140
Li Xian, Tangut emperor 140–1,
  143–6
Li Zhichang: *Journey to the
  West* 129
Liao, the 61, 80, 106
Liupan mountains 141, 142

Machiavelli, Niccolò 8
Manchu dynasty 160, 161
Mandate of Heaven *see under*
  China/Chinese
Mao Zedong 7, 8, 56, 96, 163
Mausoleum of Genghis Khan,
  nr Dongsheng 18
Mengda Beilu 81
mentors, importance of 38–9,
  134
Merkits, the 39, 44, 45–6, 58,
  168
Merv 119–121
Ming dynasty 160
Mohammed, the Prophet 41,
  56, 68, 135–6
Mohammed, shah of Khorazm
  99–100, 101, 110, 113–15,
  117–18, 121, 122
Mongol army 43–4, 51

and Baljuna Covenant 54–5,
  57
campaign against Jin 90–1,
  92, 96–7, 141, 142–3
campaign against Khorazm
  109–12, 113–18, 119–22
campaign against Xi Xia
  138–41
crossing of the Gobi 115
divisions 68
Genghis's commanders 66–8,
  112–13
on Great Raid 118–19
horseback archery 22–3
and hunts (battues) 84–5, 86,
  87–8
need for conquest 76–8
self-reliance 110–12
siege warfare 89, 91–2, 93–4,
  110, 111–12
size 66, 83, 110, 113
under Genghis's successors
  151, 153
Mongolia/Mongols 160, 161
  *anda* oath 28–9
graves 27
legal system 70–3
musical tradition 15
navy 156–7
as nomadic pastoralists 5, 21,
  22, 24–5, 84
oral records 15–16
religion 14–15, 73–4
tribal feuds 5–6, 42
writing systems 60–2, 70,
  153
  *see also* Mongol army; *Secret
    History of the Mongols, The*

Mönkhe Khan 133–5, 148, 151
Mughal empire 160
Muqali 69, 169
Muslims (Islam) 41, 125, 135
    and Genghis Khan 41, 54, 72,
        168
    and Genghis's successors 151,
        153, 159
    Mongol conquest 98–9,
        112–18
    Otrar massacre 100–2
    suicide bombers 57
    see also Mohammed, the
        Prophet
Mussolini, Benito 63

Naimans, the 58, 62, 98, 168
Nanzhao, kingdom of 152
Nestorian Christianity 40, 41,
    123, 152 and n
Nishapur 119
nökhörs 67–8, 105
Nye, Joseph S.: The Powers to
    Lead 11, 19

Ogedei Khan (Genghis's son)
    16, 104, 105, 107, 150–1
Okada, Hidehiro 161
Otrar 100–2, 115, 117, 123

Peng Daya 27
Peter Principle, the viii and n
Phags-pa (Tibetan guru) 153
Plato 125
Polo, Marco 15, 130, 148, 155
Prophet, the see Mohammed

Qilian mountains 139, 140

Quran, the 41, 116, 136

Rachewiltz, Igor de 47, 48,
    66n
Rashid al-Din 73, 142
religion(s) 71, 123–4
    see also Buddhism;
        Christianity; Daoism;
        Islam; shamanism
resilience 26–7, 30 and n
Russia 118–19, 151, 155, 159

Samarkand 99, 114, 117–18,
    131
Sasser, Earl 107
Saudi Arabia 155
Secret History of the Mongols,
    The 4, 16–17, 63, 136
    on Genghis Khan 6, 17–21,
        32, 34, 40, 52, 95, 141, 145,
        166
    on Hoelun 27–8, 32
    on Jamukha and Genghis
        43–4, 46–8, 49, 58–60, 156
    on Khasar 74
    on Mongol army 66, 68, 92
    on Muslim massacre at Otrar
        100, 102
    omissions 37, 52, 55, 112,
        115, 132, 148
    on Tangut defeat 145, 146
Shakespeare, William
    As You Like It 438
    Henry V 55
shamanism/shamans 14–15, 73,
    104, 124, 152
Shigi 52, 70, 95–6, 105–6, 169
    Blue Book 70

siege warfare 89, 91–2, 93–4,
110, 111–12
Silk Road 99
Slim, General Sir William 56–7
Song dynasty 61, 81, 82, 83, 89,
123, 143, 152, 153
Sorkan-shira 34, 35–6, 66
Subodei 69, 113, 115, 118–19,
140
Sun Zi: *Art of War* 108–9, 126
survivor personalities 29–30
Syr Dara river 113, 115

Tamerlane 159
Tanguts, the 61, 81, 88–90
*see also* Xi Xia
Tatar-Tonga 61–2, 63
Tatars, the 25, 50–2, 58, 63, 168
Taychiuts, the 25, 34, 35, 36,
52–3
Temüge (Genghis's brother) 75
Tenger (Mongol god) 14–15, 65
Three Beauties ranges 88, 139
Tibet 152–3, 160, 161
script 61
Tien Shan 98
Toghril, chief of the Kereyids
37–8, 39, 40, 41, 43–4, 45,
50–1, 58, 68, 124, 166, 167,
169
Tolui 119, 120
Tong pass 142–3

Uighurs, the 54, 62, 99, 168
writing system 62, 63, 105
United States of America 82, 114

Vietnam 12, 50, 158, 160
vision, importance of vii, 11, 42,
69–70, 167

Wansong (monk) 126
Warring States 108, 127
Weber, Max 10
Wei, Prince 83, 89, 91
Weishao, Prince 83
William (envoy from Rubrouck)
134
writing systems 60–2, 63, 70,
105, 153
Wuwei 139

Xanadu (Shang-du) 94, 155
Xi Xia empire 81, 87, 88, 110
army 82, 88
and Jin 83–4, 89, 143
Mongol campaign against
138–41, 143–8
Xinjiang 81, 153, 160, 161
Xiongnu, the (Huns) 23

Yelü Chucai 106–9, 123, 124–8,
129, 130, 133, 134, 150
*Record of a Journey to the West*
125
Yinchuan 89, 139, 140
Yisügei (Genghis's father) 25,
26, 27, 37–8, 39, 41–2
Yisügen 164
Yisui (Genghis's wife) 52, 103,
146, 164–5
Yuan dynasty 3, 159
Yunnan province 152, 153, 160